BEST POEMS ON
THE UNDERGROUND

h
t
e

BEST POEMS

ON THE

UNDERGROUND

EDITED BY

Gerard Benson · Judith Chernaik · Cicely Herbert

PHOENIX

A PHOENIX PAPERBACK

First published in Great Britain in 2009
by Weidenfeld & Nicolson
This paperback edition published in 2010
by Phoenix,
an imprint of Orion Books Ltd,
Orion House, 5 Upper St Martin's Lane,
London WC2H 9EA

An Hachette UK company

1 3 5 7 9 10 8 6 4 2

Introduction and selection © the Editors 2009
Poems copyright authors and publishers (see Acknowledgements)

A CIP catalogue record for this book
is available from the British Library.

ISBN 978-0-7538-2725-3

Typography and layout by Gwyn Lewis

Printed and bound in the UK by CPI Mackays, Chatham ME5 8TD

The Orion Publishing Group's policy is to use papers that
are natural, renewable and recyclable products and made
from wood grown in sustainable forests. The logging and
manufacturing processes are expected to conform to the
environmental regulations of the country of origin.

Poems on the Underground is registered at Companies House
in England and Wales No.06844606 as Underground Poems
Community Interest Company

www.orionbooks.co.uk

CONTENTS

INTRODUCTION

London's Poems on the Underground started life as a light-hearted idea shared among three friends, lovers of poetry and lifelong users and advocates of public transport. How pleasant it would be, we thought, if poems could be scattered among the adverts in Underground carriages. Encouraged by far-sighted Tube managers, we put together our first selection of poems, and the project was launched at Aldwych Station in January 1986.

The travelling public quickly took the project to heart. Within a short time poems had sprung up on Dublin's coastal railway, the Paris Metro, New York's vast network of subways and buses, and cities across Europe and beyond, from Moscow to Shanghai, Sydney to São Paolo. Over the past twenty years in Britain, indeed worldwide, there has been a vibrant revival in the art of poetry. We hope that our programme has played its part in this flourishing scene.

The lyric is surely one of the most perfect forms of poetry. By great good fortune, it is also ideal for display in Underground carriages, clear enough to be read easily by the traveller, brief enough, often, to commit to memory during an average Tube journey, and memorable enough to stay in the mind long after the journey is done. The reader will find many poems of this kind here in our collection, as the travelling poems return to the printed page, sometimes with missing lines and stanzas restored.

We had no idea when we began the scheme that many years later we would be offering the reading public three hundred of 'the best' poems that have since been displayed. The first five poems, all of which appear in this volume, rode the rails in

1986; they set the principles we have followed ever since. Burns and Shelley speak to readers across all barriers of time and place. William Carlos Williams, a populist American poet in the tradition of Whitman, drew on the poetry of everyday life; the Irish poet Seamus Heaney has worked to reconcile competing claims of family and history; Grace Nichols was a young Guyanese poet building a new life in Britain. The poems were from different eras and different cultures: Scots, English, American, Irish and Caribbean. This collection too draws upon past and present, from every corner of the English-speaking world.

Our original rule was to choose poems written in English, no more than fourteen lines long – sonnet length. But this meant excluding the great epics and odes of the past, and much wonderful world poetry. Rules are made to be broken and over the past twenty years we have gradually extended our boundaries to include extracts and translations along with many more delights.

Selecting three hundred 'best' poems out of the 450 displayed to date has been difficult. But there were some poems which had topical relevance at the time, no longer as urgent. Some poems depended on their context: a series of Commonwealth poems, two series of European poems with bilingual texts, three competitions for young poets. We've reluctantly omitted a number of these works. Recent series of African and Chinese poets have provided voices mainly unknown in Britain, poets we have included for that very reason. We've cut back on extracts, and have reduced the number of poems in translation. Hard choices – but we feel confident that we are offering the public a highly pleasurable anthology, with many poems that cannot be found elsewhere, and old and new, familiar and unfamiliar poems sitting alongside one another, much as they have done on the Tube. Our earlier collections included the Editors' scholarly and sometimes eccentric personal notes; sadly, we have had to omit these from Best Poems.

It is strange to think that a project that began so casually is now part of urban history, the subject of academic theses and government surveys of 'Great Art for Everyone'. We have tried to reach out to a mass public, but we've also offered poems which reflect their times and comment on them, not always in a way comfortable for officialdom. The theme of exile is recurrent, as are responses to war and peace, love and death, the nature and function of poetry – explored here in different ways by Dylan Thomas and Isaac Rosenberg, Pablo Neruda and Czeslaw Milosz, the Afghan poet Partaw Naderi and the Iraqi exile Saadi Youssef.

We have favoured the living poet, but have also trawled through the more obscure corners of the past. 'Anon' finds a place, often discovered in unique British Library manuscripts, among them 'Western wind' and several medieval carols. Much poetry starts life as song, represented here by Elizabethan madrigals and songs by Blake and Burns, Auden and Maya Angelou. London plays a central role, as home to Donne, Milton, Blake and Keats as well as émigrés and exiles. For London is the most international of cities, especially since the upheavals of the past fifty years, but also in its early days, when the Scottish poet William Dunbar praised London as 'flower of cities all'.

The alphabetical order followed here preserves the random character of the original displays, and has thrown up some unlikely and pleasing juxtapositions. Edna Millay's sonnet 'What lips my lips have kissed' introduces Spike Milligan's ode to English teeth; the 18th-century Grub Street hack Laetitia Pilkington, Swift's friend and 'Queen of the Wits', stands near the tragic figure of Sylvia Plath. Elizabeth Barrett Browning's 'Portuguese' sonnet to her husband Robert sits opposite his erotic 'Meeting at Night', to which we've added its companion piece, 'Parting at Morning'. Readers are invited to browse and to add their own choices, which they are welcome to send to us – in the hope that our programme will continue to enliven the morning rush hour.

We are greatly indebted to London Underground, now part of Transport for London, for its continued support. We are also grateful to Arts Council England, to the British Council, which distributes our poster-poems to its offices abroad, and to the Poetry Society and the Poetry Book Society, both instrumental in promoting poetry to young people and to the larger world. Our designer Tom Davidson has for several years provided a distinctive clarity and elegance for the Tube posters. Thanks also to Cassell Publishers, who first published *100 Poems on the Underground* when we had reached that magic number, and then updated the best-selling collection until it reached its 10th Edition in 2001. Weidenfeld & Nicolson expanded the collection with *New Poems on the Underground 2006*; then invited us to make a selection from the entire collection to date. Thanks finally to our patient and meticulous editor, Barry Holmes, recalled from retirement to steer the ship safely to port.

Gerard Benson, Judith Chernaik, Cicely Herbert
LONDON, 2010

THE POEMS

Mysteries

At night, I do not know who I am
when I dream, when I am sleeping.

Awakened, I hold my breath and listen:
a thumbnail scratches the other side of the wall.

At midday, I enter a sunlit room
to observe the lamplight on for no reason.

I should know by now that few octaves can be heard,
that a vision dies from being too long stared at;

that the whole of recorded history even
is but a little gossip in a great silence;

that a magnesium flash cannot illumine,
for one single moment, the invisible.

I do not complain. I start with the visible
and am startled by the visible.

DANNIE ABSE (b. 1923)

Immigrant

November '63: eight months in London.
I pause on the low bridge to watch the pelicans:
they float swanlike, arching their white necks
over only slightly ruffled bundles of wings,
burying awkward beaks in the lake's water.

I clench cold fists in my Marks and Spencer's jacket
and secretly test my accent once again:
St James's Park; St James's Park; St James's Park.

FLEUR ADCOCK (b. 1934)

Don't Call Alligator Long-Mouth
till You Cross River

Call alligator long-mouth
call alligator saw-mouth
call alligator pushy-mouth
call alligator scissors-mouth
call alligator raggedy-mouth
call alligator bumpy-bum
call alligator all dem rude word
but better wait
                    till you cross river.

JOHN AGARD (b. 1949)

The London Eye

Through my gold-tinted Gucci sunglasses,
the sightseers. Big Ben's quarter chime
strikes the convoy of number 12 buses
that bleeds into the city's monochrome.

Through somebody's zoom lens, me shouting
to you, 'Hello . . . on . . . bridge . . . 'minster!'
The aerial view postcard, the man writing
squat words like black cabs in rush hour.

The South Bank buzzes with a rising treble.
You kiss my cheek, formal as a blind date.
We enter Cupid's Capsule, a thought bubble
where I think, 'Space age!', you think, 'She was late.'

Big Ben strikes six, my SKIN. Beat blinks, replies
18.02. We're moving anti-clockwise.

PATIENCE AGBABI (b. 1965)

from Requiem

The hour of remembrance has drawn close again.
I see you, hear you, feel you:

the one they could hardly get to the window,
the one who no longer walks on this earth,

the one who shook her beautiful head,
and said: 'Coming here is like coming home.'

I would like to name them all but they took away
the list and there's no way of finding them.

For them I have woven a wide shroud
from the humble words I heard among them.

I remember them always, everywhere,
I will never forget them, whatever comes.

ANNA AKHMATOVA (1889–1966)

translated by RICHARD McKANE

Indian Cooking

The bottom of the pan was a palette –
paprika, cayenne, dhania
haldi, heaped like powder-paints.

Melted ghee made lakes, golden rivers.
The keema frying, my mother waited
for the fat to bubble to the surface.

Friends brought silver-leaf.
I dropped it on khir –
special rice pudding for parties.

I tasted the landscape, customs
of my father's country –
its fever on biting a chilli.

MONIZA ALVI (b. 1954)

Come. And Be My Baby

The highway is full of big cars
going nowhere fast
And folks is smoking anything that'll burn
Some people wrap their lives around a cocktail glass
And you sit wondering
where you're going to turn.
I got it.
Come. And be my baby.

Some prophets say the world is gonna end tomorrow
But others say we've got a week or two
The paper is full of every kind of blooming horror
And you sit wondering
what you're gonna do.
I got it.
Come. And be my baby.

MAYA ANGELOU (b. 1928)

Letter to André Billy. 9 April 1915

Gunner/Driver One (front-line)
Here I am and send you greetings
No no you're not seeing things
My Sector's number fifty-nine

I hear the whistle o_f
the   the bird
beautiful bird of pr^{e^y}

I see far away
the cathedral

```
O     D
H     E
M     A
Y  A  R
N  D  R  E
B  I  L  L  Y
```

GUILLAUME APOLLINAIRE (1880–1918)
translated by OLIVER BERNARD

The Catch

Forget
the long, smouldering
afternoon. It is

this moment
when the ball scoots
off the edge

of the bat; upwards,
backwards, falling
seemingly

beyond him
yet he reaches
and picks it

out
of its loop
like

an apple
from a branch,
the first of the season.

SIMON ARMITAGE (b. 1963)

If I Could Tell You

Time will say nothing but I told you so,
Time only knows the price we have to pay;
If I could tell you I would let you know.

If we should weep when clowns put on their show,
If we should stumble when musicians play,
Time will say nothing but I told you so.

There are no fortunes to be told, although,
Because I love you more than I can say,
If I could tell you I would let you know.

The winds must come from somewhere when they blow,
There must be reasons why the leaves decay;
Time will say nothing but I told you so.

Perhaps the roses really want to grow,
The vision seriously intends to stay;
If I could tell you I would let you know.

Suppose the lions all get up and go,
And all the brooks and soldiers run away;
Will Time say nothing but I told you so?
If I could tell you I would let you know.

W.H. AUDEN (1907–73)

Song

Stop all the clocks, cut off the telephone,
Prevent the dog from barking with a juicy bone,
Silence the pianos and with muffled drum
Bring out the coffin, let the mourners come.

Let aeroplanes circle moaning overhead
Scribbling on the sky the message He Is Dead,
Put crêpe bows round the white necks of the public doves,
Let the traffic policemen wear black cotton gloves.

He was my North, my South, my East and West,
My working week and my Sunday rest,
My noon, my midnight, my talk, my song;
I thought that love would last for ever: I was wrong.

The stars are not wanted now; put out every one,
Pack up the moon and dismantle the sun,
Pour away the ocean and sweep up the wood;
For nothing now can ever come to any good.

W.H. AUDEN

In the Heart of Hackney

for Aidan Andrew Dun

Behold, a swan. Ten houseboats on the Lee.
   A cyclist on the towpath. Gentle rain.
A pigeon in a white apple-blossoming tree.
   And through the Marsh the rumble of a train.

Two courting geese waddle on the bank
   Croaking. A man unties his boat.
Police cars howl and whoop. And vast and blank
   The rain cloud of the sky is trampled underfoot.

Behold, a dove. And in Bomb Crater Pond
   Fat frogs ignore the rain.
Each trembling rush signals like a wand
   Earthing the magic of London once again.

In the heart of Hackney, five miles from Kentish Town,
By Lammas Lands the reed beds are glowing rich and brown.

SEBASTIAN BARKER (b. 1945)

'Autumn evening'

Autumn evening –
A crow on a bare branch.

MATSUO BASHŌ (1644–94)
translated by KENNETH REXROTH

'Autumn evening' Calligraphy by
Yukki Yaura, specially commissioned
from the artist by Poems on the
Underground. © Yukki Yaura 2004.

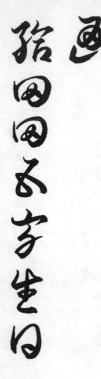

A Picture *

for Tiantian's fifth birthday

Morning arrives in a sleeveless dress
apples tumble all over the earth
my daughter is drawing a picture
how vast is a five-year-old sky
your name has two windows
one opens towards a sun with no clock-hands
the other opens towards your father
who has become a hedgehog in exile
taking with him a few unintelligible characters
and a bright red apple
he has left your painting
how vast is a five-year-old sky

BEI DAO (b. 1949)
translated by BONNIE S. McDOUGALL
and CHEN MAIPING

*Tiantian, the nickname given to the poet's daughter, is written with
two characters which look like a pair of windows. The same character
also forms a part of the character for the word 'picture'.

Calligraphy by Yukki Yaura © Yukki Yaura 1993.

Shopper

I am spending my way out
of a recession. The road chokes
on delivery vans.

I used to be Just Looking Round,
I used to be How Much, and
Have You Got it in Beige.

Now I devour whole stores –
high speed spin; giant size; chunky gold;
de luxe springing. Things.

I drag them round me into a stockade.
It is dark inside; but my credit cards
are incandescent.

CONNIE BENSLEY (b. 1929)

The Coming of Grendel

Now from the marshlands under the mist-mountains
Came Grendel prowling; branded with God's ire.
This murderous monster was minded to entrap
Some hapless human in that high hall.
On he came under the clouds, until clearly
He could see the great golden feasting place,
Glimmering wine-hall of men. Not his first
Raid was this on the homeplace of Hrothgar.
Never before though and never afterward
Did he encounter hardier defenders of a hall.

from BEOWULF (10th century or earlier)
translated by GERARD BENSON

Benediction

Thanks to the ear
that someone may hear

Thanks to seeing
that someone may see

Thanks to feeling
that someone may feel

Thanks to touch
that one may be touched

Thanks to flowering of white moon
and spreading shawl of black night
holding villages and cities together

JAMES BERRY (b. 1924)

City

When the great bell
BOOMS over the Portland stone urn, and
From the carved cedar wood
Rises the odour of incense,
I SIT DOWN
In St. Botolph Bishopsgate Churchyard
And wait for the spirit of my grandfather
Toddling along from the Barbican.

JOHN BETJEMAN (1906–84)

Drawing by David Gentleman, commissioned by
Poems on the Underground

Love in a Bathtub

Years later we'll remember the bathtub,
the position
            of the taps
the water, slippery
as if a bucketful
            of eels had joined us . . .
we'll be old, our children grown up
but we'll remember the water
                        sloshing out
the useless soap,
the mountain of wet towels.
'Remember the bathtub in Belfast?'
we'll prod each other –

SUJATA BHATT (b. 1956)

giovanni caboto/john cabot

fourteen hundred and ninety seven
giovanni sailed from the coast of devon

    52 days   discovered cape breton n.s.
    caught some cod   went home
    with 10 bear hides
    (none prime)

    told henry 7
    his majesty now owned
    cipango   land of jewels
    abounding moreover in silks
    & brasilwode
    also the spice islands of asia
    & the country of the grand khan

    henry gave giovanni 30 quid
    to go back to nova scotia

who was kidding who?

EARLE BIRNEY (1904–95)

One Art

The art of losing isn't hard to master;
so many things seem filled with the intent
to be lost that their loss is no disaster.

Lose something every day. Accept the fluster
of lost door keys, the hour badly spent.
The art of losing isn't hard to master.

Then practice losing farther, losing faster:
places, and names, and where it was you meant
to travel. None of these will bring disaster.

I lost my mother's watch. And look! my last, or
next-to-last, of three loved houses went.
The art of losing isn't hard to master.

I lost two cities, lovely ones. And, vaster,
some realms I owned, two rivers, a continent.
I miss them, but it wasn't a disaster.

– Even losing you (the joking voice, a gesture
I love) I shan't have lied. It's evident
the art of losing's not too hard to master
though it may look like (*Write* it!) like disaster.

ELIZABETH BISHOP (1911–79)

The Tyger

Tyger Tyger, burning bright,
In the forests of the night;
What immortal hand or eye,
Could frame thy fearful symmetry?

In what distant deeps or skies
Burnt the fire of thine eyes!
On what wings dare he aspire?
What the hand, dare sieze the fire?

And what shoulder, & what art,
Could twist the sinews of thy heart?
And when thy heart began to beat,
What dread hand? & what dread feet?

What the hammer? what the chain?
In what furnace was thy brain?
What the anvil? what dread grasp,
Dare its deadly terrors clasp?

When the stars threw down their spears
And water'd heaven with their tears:
Did he smile his work to see?
Did he who made the Lamb make thee?

Tyger Tyger, burning bright,
In the forests of the night:
What immortal hand or eye,
Dare frame thy fearful symmetry?

WILLIAM BLAKE (1757–1827)

The Sick Rose

O Rose thou art sick.
The invisible worm
That flies in the night
In the howling storm,

Has found out thy bed
Of crimson joy:
And his dark secret love
Does thy life destroy.

WILLIAM BLAKE

Ah! Sun-flower

Ah! Sun-flower, weary of time,
Who countest the steps of the Sun,
Seeking after that sweet golden clime
Where the traveller's journey is done,

Where the Youth pined away with desire
And the pale Virgin shrouded in snow
Arise from their graves and aspire
Where my Sun-flower wishes to go.

WILLIAM BLAKE

Sun a-shine an' rain a-fall,
The Devil an' him wife cyan 'gree at all,
The two o' them want one fish-head,
The Devil call him wife bonehead,
She hiss her teeth, call him cock-eye,
Greedy, worthless an' workshy,
While them busy callin' name,
The puss walk in, sey is a shame
To see a nice fish go to was'e,
Lef' with a big grin pon him face.

VALERIE BLOOM (b. 1956)

Sun a-shine, rain a-fall   Illustration by Michael Charlton.

The Emigrant Irish

Like oil lamps we put them out the back,

of our houses, of our minds. We had lights
better than, newer than and then

a time came, this time and now
we need them. Their dread, makeshift example.

They would have thrived on our necessities.
What they survived we could not even live.
By their lights now it is time to
imagine how they stood there, what they stood with,
that their possessions may become our power.

Cardboard. Iron. Their hardships parcelled in them.
Patience. Fortitude. Long-suffering
in the bruise-coloured dusk of the New World.

And all the old songs. And nothing to lose.

EAVAN BOLAND (b. 1944)

'Let a place be made'

Let a place be made for the one who draws near,
The one who is cold, deprived of any home,

Tempted by the sound of a lamp, by the lit
Threshold of a solitary house.

And if he is still exhausted, full of anguish,
Say again for him those words that heal.

What does this heart which once was silence need
If not those words which are both sign and prayer,

Like a fire caught sight of in the sudden night,
Like the table glimpsed in a poor house?

YVES BONNEFOY (b. 1923)
translated by ANTHONY RUDOLF

To My Dear and Loving Husband

If ever two were one, then surely we.
If ever man were loved by wife, then thee;
If ever wife was happy in a man,
Compare with me ye women if you can.
I prize thy love more than whole mines of gold,
Or all the riches that the East doth hold.
My love is such that rivers cannot quench,
Nor aught but love from thee give recompence.
Thy love is such I can no way repay,
The heavens reward thee manifold I pray.
Then while we live, in love let's so persever,
That when we live no more, we may live ever.

ANNE BRADSTREET (1612–72)

Naima

for John Coltrane

Propped against the crowded bar
he pours into the curved and silver horn
his old unhappy longing for a home

the dancers twist and turn
he leans and wishes he could burn
his memories to ashes like some old notorious emperor

of rome. but no stars blazed across the sky when he
   was born
no wise men found his hovel. this crowded bar
   where dancers twist and turn

holds all the fame and recognition he will ever earn
on earth or heaven. he leans against the bar
and pours his old unhappy longing in the saxophone

KAMAU BRATHWAITE (b. 1930)

Moonwise

(for my children, all)

sometimes
you know
the moon
is not such a perfect
circle

and the master Painter
makes a passing
brush touch
with a cloud

don't worry
we've passed
the dark side

all you children
rest easy now

we are born

moonwise

JEAN 'BINTA' BREEZE (b. 1956)

In the Poem

To bring the picture the wall the wind
The flower the glass the shine on wood
And the cold chaste clearness of water
To the clean severe world of the poem

To save from death decay and ruin
The actual moment of vision and surprise
And keep in the real world
The real gesture of a hand touching the table.

SOPHIA DE MELLO BREYNER (1919–2004)
translated by RUTH FAINLIGHT

The Poet

Therefore he no more troubled the pool of silence.
But put on mask and cloak,
Strung a guitar
And moved among the folk.
Dancing they cried,
'Ah, how our sober islands
Are gay again, since this blind lyrical tramp
Invaded the Fair!'

Under the last dead lamp
When all the dancers and masks had gone inside
His cold stare
Returned to its true task, interrogation of silence.

GEORGE MACKAY BROWN (1921–96)

Sonnet from the Portuguese

How do I love thee? Let me count the ways.
I love thee to the depth and breadth and height
My soul can reach, when feeling out of sight
For the ends of Being and ideal Grace.
I love thee to the level of everyday's
Most quiet need, by sun and candlelight.
I love thee freely, as men strive for Right;
I love thee purely, as they turn from Praise.
I love thee with the passion put to use
In my old griefs, and with my childhood's faith.
I love thee with a love I seemed to lose
With my lost saints, – I love thee with the breath,
Smiles, tears, of all my life! – and, if God choose,
I shall but love thee better after death.

ELIZABETH BARRETT BROWNING (1806–61)

Meeting at Night

The grey sea and the long black land;
And the yellow half-moon large and low;
And the startled little waves that leap
In fiery ringlets from their sleep,
As I gain the cove with pushing prow,
And quench its speed i' the slushy sand.

Then a mile of warm sea-scented beach;
Three fields to cross till a farm appears;
A tap at the pane, the quick sharp scratch
And blue spurt of a lighted match,
And a voice less loud, thro' its joys and fears,
Than the two hearts beating each to each!

ROBERT BROWNING (1812–89)

Parting at Morning

Round the cape of a sudden came the sea,
And the sun looked over the mountain's rim:
And straight was a path of gold for him,
And the need of a world of men for me.

ROBERT BROWNING

Home-Thoughts, from Abroad

I

Oh, to be in England
Now that April's there,
And whoever wakes in England
Sees, some morning, unaware,
That the lowest boughs and the brushwood sheaf
Round the elm-tree bole are in tiny leaf,
While the chaffinch sings on the orchard bough
In England – now!

II

And after April, when May follows,
And the whitethroat builds, and all the swallows!
Hark, where my blossomed pear-tree in the hedge
Leans to the field and scatters on the clover
Blossoms and dewdrops – at the bent spray's edge –
That's the wise thrush; he sings each song twice over,
Lest you should think he never could recapture
The first fine careless rapture!
And though the fields look rough with hoary dew,
All will be gay when noontide wakes anew
The buttercups, the little children's dower
– Far brighter than this gaudy melon-flower!

ROBERT BROWNING

Personal Column

… As to my heart, that may as well be forgotten
or labelled: Owner will dispose of same
to a good home, refs. exchgd., h.&c.,
previous experience desired but not essential
or let on a short lease to suit convenience.

BASIL BUNTING (1900–85)

Up in the Morning Early

Cauld blaws the wind frae east to west,
  The drift is driving sairly;
Sae loud and shrill's I hear the blast,
  I'm sure it's winter fairly.

CHORUS: Up in the morning's no for me,
  Up in the morning early;
When a' the hills are cover'd wi' snaw,
  I'm sure it's winter fairly.

The birds sit chittering in the thorn,
  A' day they fare but sparely;
And lang's the night frae e'en to morn,
  I'm sure it's winter fairly.

CHORUS: Up in the morning's no for me,
  Up in the morning early;
When a' the hills are cover'd wi' snaw,
  I'm sure it's winter fairly.

ROBERT BURNS (1759–96)

A red red Rose

O my Luve's like a red, red rose,
   That's newly sprung in June;
O my Luve's like the melodie
   That's sweetly play'd in tune.

As fair art thou, my bonnie lass,
   So deep in luve am I;
And I will love thee still, my Dear,
   Till a' the seas gang dry.

Till a' the seas gang dry, my Dear,
   And the rocks melt wi' the sun:
I will love thee still, my Dear,
   While the sands o' life shall run.

And fare thee weel, my only Luve!
   And fare thee weel, a while!
And I will come again, my Luve,
   Tho' it were ten thousand mile!

ROBERT BURNS

A Private Life

I want to drive home in the dusk
of some late afternoon,

the journey slow, the tractors spilling hay,
the land immense and bright, like memory,

the pit towns smudges of graphite,
their names scratched out for good: Lumphinnans;

Kelty. I want to see
the darkened rooms, the cups and wireless sets,

the crimson lamps across the playing fields,
the soft men walking home through streets and parks

and quiet women, coming to their doors,
then turning away, their struck lives gathered around them.

JOHN BURNSIDE (b. 1955)

'So we'll go no more a-roving'

So we'll go no more a-roving
   So late into the night,
Though the heart be still as loving,
   And the moon be still as bright.

For the sword outwears its sheath,
   And the soul wears out the breast,
And the heart must pause to breathe,
   And Love itself have rest.

Though the night was made for loving,
   And the day returns too soon,
Yet we'll go no more a-roving
   By the light of the moon.

GEORGE GORDON, LORD BYRON (1788–1824)

Caedmon's Hymn

Now we must praise to the skies the Keeper of the
    heavenly kingdom,
The might of the Measurer, all he has in mind,
The work of the Father of Glory, of all manner
    of marvel,

Our eternal Master, the main mover.
It was he who first summoned up, on our behalf,
Heaven as a roof, the holy Maker.

Then this middle-earth, the Watcher over humankind,
Our eternal Master, would later assign
The precinct of men, the Lord Almighty.

from Bede's HISTORY (*7th century AD*)

translated by PAUL MULDOON

'Now winter nights enlarge'

Now winter nights enlarge
   The number of their hours
And clouds their storms discharge
   Upon the airy towers.
Let now the chimneys blaze,
   And cups o'erflow with wine:
Let well-tun'd words amaze
   With harmony divine.
Now yellow waxen lights
   Shall wait on honey Love,
While youthful Revels, Masks, and Courtly sights,
   Sleep's leaden spells remove.

This time doth well dispense
   With lovers' long discourse;
Much speech hath some defence,
   Though beauty no remorse.
All do not all things well;
   Some measures comely tread;
Some knotted Riddles tell;
   Some Poems smoothly read.
The Summer hath his joys,
   And Winter his delights;
Though Love and all his pleasures are but toys,
   They shorten tedious nights.

THOMAS CAMPION (1567–1620)

On Lake Nicaragua

Slow cargo-launch, midnight, mid-lake,
bound from San Miguelito to Granada.
The lights ahead not yet in sight,
the dwindling ones behind completely gone.
Only the stars
(the mast a finger pointing to the Seven Sisters)
     and the moon, rising above Chontales.

Another launch (just one red light) goes by
and sinks into the night.
We, for them:
     another red light sinking in the night...
And I, watching the stars, lying on the deck
between bunches of bananas and Chontales cheeses,
wonder: perhaps there's one that is an earth like ours
and someone's watching me (watching the stars)
from another launch, on another night, on another lake.

ERNESTO CARDENAL (b. 1925)

translated by ERNESTO CARDENAL *and* ROBERT PRING-MILL

Father William

'You are old, father William,' the young man said,
    'And your hair is exceedingly white:
And yet you incessantly stand on your head –
    Do you think, at your age, it is right?'

'In my youth,' father William replied to his son,
    'I feared it *might* injure the brain:
But now that I'm perfectly sure I have none,
    Why, I do it again and again.'

'You are old,' said the youth, 'as I mentioned before,
    And have grown most uncommonly fat:
Yet you turned a back-somersault in at the door –
    Pray what is the reason of that?'

'In my youth,' said the sage, as he shook his gray locks,
    'I kept all my limbs very supple
By the use of this ointment, five shillings the box –
    Allow me to sell you a couple.'

'You are old,' said the youth, 'and your jaws are too weak
    For anything tougher than suet:
Yet you eat all the goose, with the bones and the beak –
    Pray, how did you manage to do it?'

'In my youth,' said the old man, 'I took to the law,
    And argued each case with my wife,
And *the muscular strength, which it gave to my jaw*,
    Has lasted the rest of my life.'

'You are old,' said the youth, 'one would hardly suppose
     That your eye was as steady as ever:
Yet you balanced an eel on the end of your nose –
     What made you so *awfully* clever?'

'I have answered three questions, and that is enough,'
     Said his father, 'don't give yourself airs!
Do you think I can listen all day to such stuff?
     Be off, or I'll kick you down stairs!'

LEWIS CARROLL (1832–98)

Father William   From the author's manuscript copy of *Alice's Adventures Under Ground*. By permission of The British Library Board.

Return to Cornwall

I think no longer of the antique city
  Of Pompey and the red-haired Alexander.
The brilliant harbour, the wrecked light at Pharos,
  Are buried deep with Mediterranean plunder.

Here, by the Inney, nature has her city:
  (O the cypress trees of Mahomed Ali Square!)
The children build their harbour in the meadow
  And the crystal lark floats on the Cornish air.

CHARLES CAUSLEY (1917–2003)

'Thread suns'

Thread suns
above the grey-black wilderness.
A tree-
high thought
tunes in to light's pitch: there are
still songs to be sung on the other side
of mankind.

PAUL CELAN (1920–70)
translated by MICHAEL HAMBURGER

What He Said

What could my mother be
to yours? What kin is my father
to yours anyway? And how
did you and I meet ever?
            But in love
our hearts have mingled
like red earth and pouring rain.

CEMPULAPPEYANIRAR
(1st–3rd century AD)
translated by A.K. RAMANUJAN

What He Said A traditional
Tamil design. By permission of
Gowri Ramnarayan.

Viv

for cricketer, Vivian Richards

Like the sun rising and setting
Like the thunderous roar of a bull rhino
Like the sleek, quick grace of a gazelle,
The player springs into the eye
And lights the world with fires
Of a million dreams, a million aspirations.
The batsman-hero climbs the skies,
Strikes the earth-ball for six
And the landscape rolls with the ecstasy of the magic play.

Through the covers, the warrior thrusts a majestic cut
Lighting the day with runs
As bodies reel and tumble,
Hands clap, eyes water
And hearts move inside out.

The volcano erupts!
Blows the game apart.

FAUSTIN CHARLES (b. 1944)

Two Roundels
'Now welcome Summer'

Now welcome Summer with thy sunnė soft,
That hast this winter's weathers overshake,
And driven away the longė nightės black.

Saint Valentine, that art full high aloft,
Thus singen smallė fowlės for thy sake:
Now welcome Summer with thy sunnė soft,
That hast this winter's weathers overshake.

Well have they cause for to gladden oft,
Since each of them recovered hath his make.
Full blissful may they singė when they wake:
Now welcome Summer with thy sunnė soft,
That hast this winter's weathers overshake,
And driven away the longė nightės black!

from THE PARLIAMENT OF FOWLS

GEOFFREY CHAUCER (1340?–1400)

Since I from Love escaped am so fat,
I never think to be in his prison lean;
Since I am free, I count him not a bean.

He may answer and say right this and that;
I do no force, I speak right as I mean.
Since I from Love escaped am so fat,
I never think to be in his prison lean.

Love hath my name stricken out of his slate,
And he is struck out of my bookės clean
For ever more, there is no other mean.
Since I from Love escaped am so fat,
I never think to be in his prison lean;
Since I am free, I count him not a bean.

GEOFFREY CHAUCER

I do no force: I care not

Tortoise

Under the mottled shell of the old tortoise
beats the heart of a young dancer.

She dreams of twirling on table-tops,
turning cartwheels,
kicking up her heels at the Carnival ball.

'Oh, who will kiss my cold and wrinkled lips,
and set my dreaming spirit free?'

JUDITH CHERNAIK (b. 1934)

Illustration by Satoshi Kitamura

Swineherd

When all this is over, said the swineherd,
I mean to retire, where
Nobody will have heard about my special skills
And conversation is mainly about the weather.

I intend to learn how to make coffee, at least as well
As the Portuguese lay-sister in the kitchen
And polish the brass fenders every day.
I want to lie awake at night
Listening to cream crawling to the top of the jug
And the water lying soft in the cistern.

I want to see an orchard where the trees grow in straight
lines
And the yellow fox finds shelter between the navy-blue
trunks,
Where it gets dark early in summer
And the apple-blossom is allowed to wither on the bough.

EILÉAN NÍ CHUILLEANÁIN (b. 1942)

Content

Like walking in fog, in fog and mud,
do you remember, love? We kept,
for once, to the tourist path, boxed in mist,
conscious of just our feet and breath,
and at the peak, sat hand in hand, and let
the cliffs we'd climbed and cliffs to come
reveal themselves and be veiled again
quietly, with the prevailing wind.

KATE CLANCHY (b. 1965)

Emmonsails Heath in Winter

I love to see the old heaths withered brake
Mingle its crimpled leaves with furze and ling
While the old heron from the lonely lake
Starts slow and flaps his melancholly wing
And oddling crow in idle motions swing
On the half rotten ash trees topmost twig
Beside whose trunk the gipsey makes his bed
Up flies the bouncing woodcock from the brig
Where a black quagmire quakes beneath the tread
The fieldfare chatters in the whistling thorn
And for the awe round fields and closen rove
And coy bumbarrels twenty in a drove
Flit down the hedgerows in the frozen plain
And hang on little twigs and start again

JOHN CLARE (1793–1864)

awe: haw   *bumbarrels:* long-tailed tits   *closen:* small enclosed fields

I Am

I am – yet what I am none cares or knows,
My friends forsake me like a memory lost;
I am the self-consumer of my woes,
They rise and vanish in oblivious host
Like shades in love and death's oblivion lost,
And yet I am – and live, with shadows tossed

Into the nothingness of scorn and noise,
Into the living sea of waking dreams,
Where there is neither sense of life nor joys,
But the vast shipwreck of my life's esteems;
And e'en the dearest, that I loved the best,
Are strange – nay, rather stranger than the rest.

I long for scenes where man has never trod,
A place where woman never smiled or wept,
There to abide with my creator, God,
And sleep as I in childhood sweetly slept,
Untroubling and untroubled where I lie;
The grass below – above the vaulted sky.

JOHN CLARE

Taid's Grave

Rain on lilac leaves. In the dusk
they show me the grave,
a casket of stars underfoot,
his name there, and his language.

Voice of thrushes in rain.
My cousin Gwynfor eases me
into the green cave.
Wet hands of lilac

touch my wrist and the secret
unfreckled underside of my arm
daring fingers to count
five warm blue eggs.

GILLIAN CLARKE (b. 1937)

Taid: Welsh for grandfather

from Frost at Midnight

The Frost performs its secret ministry,
Unhelped by any wind. The owlet's cry
Came loud – and hark, again! loud as before.
The inmates of my cottage, all at rest,
Have left me to that solitude, which suits
Abstruser musings: save that at my side
My cradled infant slumbers peacefully.
'Tis calm indeed! so calm, that it disturbs
And vexes meditation with its strange
And extreme silentness. Sea, hill, and wood,
This populous village! Sea, and hill, and wood,
With all the numberless goings-on of life,
Inaudible as dreams!

SAMUEL TAYLOR COLERIDGE (1772–1834)

Coltsfoot and Larches

I love coltsfoot that they
Make their appearance into life among dead grass:
Larches, that they
Die colourfully among sombre immortals.

DAVID CONSTANTINE (b. 1944)

Bowl

Give me a bowl, wide
and shallow. Patient
to light as a landscape open
to the whole weight
of a deepening sky.

Give me a bowl which turns
for ever on a curve
so gentle a child
could bear it and beasts
lap fearless at its low rim.

ELIZABETH COOK (b. 1952)

The Uncertainty of the Poet

I am a poet.
I am very fond of bananas.

I am bananas.
I am very fond of a poet.

I am a poet of bananas.
I am very fond.

A fond poet of 'I am, I am' –
Very bananas.

Fond of 'Am I bananas?
Am I?' – a very poet.

Bananas of a poet!
Am I fond? Am I very?

Poet bananas! I am.
I am fond of a 'very'.

I am of very fond bananas.
Am I a poet?

WENDY COPE (b. 1945)

Parting in Wartime

How long ago Hector took off his plume
Not wanting that his little son should cry,
Then kissed his sad Andromache goodbye –
And now we three in Euston waiting-room.

FRANCES CORNFORD (1886–1960)

from The Borough

High o'er the restless deep, above the reach
Of gunner's hope, vast flights of wild ducks stretch;
Far as the eye can glance on either side,
In a broad space and level line they glide;
All in their wedge-like figures from the north,
Day after day, flight after flight go forth.
   In-shore their passage tribes of sea-gulls urge,
And drop for prey within the sweeping surge;
Oft in the rough opposing blast they fly
Far back, then turn and all their force apply,
While to the storm they give their weak complaining cry;
Or clap the sleek white pinion to the breast,
And in the restless ocean dip for rest.

– Letter 1, lines 218–230

GEORGE CRABBE (1754–1832)

'I saw a man pursuing the horizon'

I saw a man pursuing the horizon;
Round and round they sped.
I was disturbed at this;
I accosted the man.
'It is futile,' I said,
'You can never—'

'You lie,' he cried,
And ran on.

STEPHEN CRANE (1871–1900)

The Cries of London

Here's fine rosemary, sage, and thyme.
Come buy my ground ivy.
Here's fetherfew, gilliflowers and rue.
Come buy my knotted marjorum, ho!
Come buy my mint, my fine green mint.
Here's fine lavender for your cloaths.
Here's parsley and winter-savory,
And hearts-ease, which all do choose.
Here's balm and hissop, and cinquefoil,
All fine herbs, it is well known.
    Let none despise the merry, merry cries
    Of famous London-town!

Here's fine herrings, eight a groat.
Hot codlins, pies and tarts.
New mackerel! have to sell.
Come buy my Wellfleet oysters, ho!
Come buy my whitings fine and new.
Wives, shall I mend your husbands horns?
I'll grind your knives to please your wives,
And very nicely cut your corns.
Maids, have you any hair to sell,
Either flaxen, black, or brown?
    Let none despise the merry, merry cries
    Of famous London-town!

ANON. (17th century)

Anglo-Saxon Riddle

I'm a strange creature, for I satisfy women,
a service to the neighbours! No one suffers
at my hands except for my slayer.
I grow very tall, erect in a bed,
I'm hairy underneath. From time to time
a good-looking girl, the doughty daughter
of some churl dares to hold me,
grips my russet skin, robs me of my head
and puts me in the pantry. At once that girl
with plaited hair who has confined me
remembers our meeting. Her eye moistens.

from THE EXETER BOOK

ANON. (before 1000)
translated by KEVIN CROSSLEY-HOLLAND

Suggested answer: Onion

Mama Dot

Born on a sunday
in the kingdom of Ashante

Sold on monday
into slavery

Ran away on tuesday
cause she born free

Lost a foot on wednesday
when they catch she

Worked all thursday
till her head grey

Dropped on friday
where they burned she

Freed on saturday
in a new century

FRED D'AGUIAR (b. 1960)

Rondel

The weather's cast its cloak of grey
Woven of wind and cold and rain,
And wears embroidered clothes again
Of clear sunshine, in fair array.

No beast, no bird, but in its way
Cries out or sings in wood and plain:
The weather's cast its cloak of grey
Woven of wind and cold and rain.

River and spring and brook this day
Wear handsome liveries that feign
More silver stars than Charles's Wain,
Mingled with drops of golden spray.
The weather's cast its cloak of grey.

CHARLES D'ORLÉANS (1394–1465)
translated by OLIVER BERNARD

Silver

Slowly, silently, now the moon
Walks the night in her silver shoon;
This way, and that, she peers, and sees
Silver fruit upon silver trees;
One by one the casements catch
Her beams beneath the silvery thatch;
Couched in his kennel, like a log,
With paws of silver sleeps the dog;
From their shadowy cote the white breasts peep
Of doves in a silver-feathered sleep;
A harvest mouse goes scampering by,
With silver claws, and silver eye;
And moveless fish in the water gleam
By silver reeds in a silver stream.

WALTER DE LA MARE (1873–1956)

Canticle

Sometimes when you walk down to the red gate
hearing the scrape-music of your shoes across gravel,
a yellow moon will lift over the hill;
you swing the gate shut and lean on the topmost bar
as if something has been accomplished in the world;
a night wind mistles through the poplar leaves
and all the noise of the universe stills
to an oboe hum, the given note of a perfect
music; there is a vast sky wholly dedicated
to the stars and you know, with certainty,
that all the dead are out, up there, in one
holiday flotilla, and that they celebrate
the fact of a red gate and a yellow moon
that tunes their instruments with you to the symphony.

JOHN F. DEANE (b. 1943)

Cradle Song

Golden slumbers kiss your eyes,
Smiles awake you when you rise;
Sleep, pretty wantons, do not cry,
And I will sing a lullaby,
Rock them, rock them, lullaby.

Care is heavy, therefore sleep you,
You are care, and care must keep you;
Sleep, pretty wantons, do not cry,
And I will sing a lullaby,
Rock them, rock them, lullaby.

THOMAS DEKKER (1570–1632)

Should You Die First

Let me at least collect your smells
as specimens: your armpits, woollen sweater,
fingers yellow from smoke. I'd need
to take an imprint of your foot
and make recordings of your laugh.

These archives I shall carry into exile;
my body a St Helena where ships no longer dock,
a rock in the ocean, an outpost where the wind howls
and polar bears beat down the door.

ANNABELLE DESPARD (b. 1943)

The Language Issue

I place my hope on the water
in this little boat
of the language, the way a body might put
an infant

in a basket of intertwined
iris leaves,
its underside proofed
with bitumen and pitch,

then set the whole thing down amidst
the sedge
and bulrushes by the edge
of a river

only to have it borne hither and thither,
not knowing where it might end up;
in the lap, perhaps,
of some Pharaoh's daughter.

NUALA NÍ DHOMHNAILL (b. 1952)
translated from the Irish by PAUL MULDOON

74

'I taste a liquor never brewed'

I taste a liquor never brewed –
From Tankards scooped in Pearl –
Not all the Vats upon the Rhine
Yield such an Alcohol!

Inebriate of Air – am I –
And Debauchee of Dew –
Reeling – thro endless summer days –
From inns of Molten Blue –

When 'Landlords' turn the drunken Bee
Out of the Foxglove's door –
When Butterflies – renounce their 'drams' –
I shall but drink the more!

Till Seraphs swing their snowy Hats –
And Saints – to windows run –
To see the little Tippler
Leaning against the – Sun –

EMILY DICKINSON (1830–86)

'I stepped from Plank to Plank'

I stepped from Plank to Plank
A slow and cautious way
The Stars about my Head I felt
About my Feet the Sea.

I knew not but the next
Would be my final inch –
This gave me that precarious Gait
Some call Experience.

EMILY DICKINSON

'Much Madness is divinest Sense'

Much Madness is divinest Sense –
To a discerning Eye –
Much Sense – the starkest Madness –
'Tis the Majority
In this, as All, prevail –
Assent – and you are sane –
Demur – you're straightway dangerous –
And handled with a Chain –

EMILY DICKINSON

The Present

For the present there is just one moon,
though every level pond gives back another.

But the bright disc shining in the black lagoon,
perceived by astrophysicist and lover,

is milliseconds old. And even that light's
seven minutes older than its source.

And the stars we think we see on moonless nights
are long extinguished. And, of course,

this very moment, as you read this line,
is literally gone before you know it.

Forget the here-and-now. We have no time
but this device of wantonness and wit.

Make me this present then: your hand in mine,
and we'll live out our lives in it.

MICHAEL DONAGHY (1954–2004)

The Good Morrow

I wonder, by my troth, what thou and I
Did, till we loved; were we not weaned till then,
But sucked on country pleasures, childishly?
Or snorted we in the Seven Sleepers' den?
'Twas so; but this, all pleasures fancies be.
If ever any beauty I did see,
Which I desired, and got, 'twas but a dream of thee.

And now good morrow to our waking souls,
Which watch not one another out of fear;
For love, all love of other sights controls,
And makes one little room, an everywhere.
Let sea-discoverers to new worlds have gone,
Let maps to others, worlds on worlds have shown,
Let us possess our world; each hath one, and is one.

My face in thine eye, thine in mine appears,
And true plain hearts do in the faces rest;
Where can we find two better hemispheres,
Without sharp North, without declining West?
Whatever dies, was not mixed equally;
If our two loves be one; or thou and I
Love so alike that none do slacken, none can die.

JOHN DONNE (1572–1631)

Holy Sonnet

Death be not proud, though some have called thee
Mighty and dreadful, for thou art not so;
For those whom thou think'st thou dost overthrow
Die not, poor death, nor yet canst thou kill me.
From rest and sleep, which but thy pictures be,
Much pleasure, then from thee much more must flow;
And soonest our best men with thee do go,
Rest of their bones, and souls' delivery.
Thou art slave to Fate, chance, kings, and desperate men,
And dost with poison, war, and sickness dwell,
And poppy or charms can make us sleep as well,
And better than thy stroke; why swell'st thou then?
One short sleep past, we wake eternally,
And death shall be no more, Death thou shalt die.

JOHN DONNE

Letters from Yorkshire

In February, digging his garden, planting potatoes,
he saw the first lapwings return and came
indoors to write to me, his knuckles singing

as they reddened in the warmth.
It's not romance, simply how things are.
You out there, in the cold, seeing the seasons

turning, me with my heartful of headlines
feeding words onto a blank screen.
Is your life more real because you dig and sow?

You wouldn't say so, breaking ice on a waterbutt,
clearing a path through snow. Still, it's you
who sends me word of that other world

pouring air and light into an envelope. So that
at night, watching the same news in different houses,
our souls tap out messages across the icy miles.

MAURA DOOLEY (b. 1957)

Notes from a Tunisian Journal

This nutmeg stick of a boy in loose trousers!
Little coffee pots in the coals, a mint on the tongue.

The camels stand in all their vague beauty –
at night they fold up like pale accordions.

All the hedges are singing with yellow birds!
A boy runs by with lemons in his hands.

Food's perfume, breath is nourishment.
The stars crumble, salt above eucalyptus fields.

RITA DOVE (b. 1952)

They Are Not Long

Vitae summa brevis spem nos vetat incohare longam*

They are not long, the weeping and the laughter,
    Love and desire and hate:
I think they have no portion in us after
    We pass the gate.

They are not long, the days of wine and roses:
    Out of a misty dream
Our path emerges for a while, then closes
    Within a dream.

ERNEST DOWSON (1867–1900)

*Life's short span prevents us from entertaining far-off hopes (Horace)

'Since there's no help, come let us kiss and part'

Since there's no help, come let us kiss and part,
Nay, I have done: you get no more of me,
And I am glad, yea glad with all my heart
That thus so cleanly I myself can free,
Shake hands for ever, cancel all our vows,
And when we meet at any time again,
Be it not seen in either of our brows
That we one jot of former love retain.
Now at the last gasp of love's latest breath,
When his pulse failing, passion speechless lies,
When faith is kneeling by his bed of death,
And innocence is closing up his eyes,
    Now if thou wouldst, when all have given him over,
    From death to life thou might'st him yet recover.

MICHAEL DRAYTON (1563–1631)

Words, Wide Night

Somewhere on the other side of this wide night
and the distance between us, I am thinking of you.
The room is turning slowly away from the moon.

This is pleasurable. Or shall I cross that out and say
it is sad? In one of the tenses I singing
an impossible song of desire that you cannot hear.

La lala la. See? I close my eyes and imagine
the dark hills I would have to cross
to reach you. For I am in love with you and this

is what it is like or what it is like in words.

CAROL ANN DUFFY (b. 1955)

Prayer

Some days, although we cannot pray, a prayer
utters itself. So, a woman will lift
her head from the sieve of her hands and stare
at the minims sung by a tree, a sudden gift.

Some nights, although we are faithless, the truth
enters our hearts, that small familiar pain;
then a man will stand stock-still, hearing his youth
in the distant Latin chanting of a train.

Pray for us now. Grade I piano scales
console the lodger looking out across
a Midlands town. Then dusk, and someone calls
a child's name as though they named their loss.

Darkness outside. Inside, the radio's prayer –
Rockall. Malin. Dogger. Finisterre.

CAROL ANN DUFFY

To the City of London

London, thou art of towns *A per se*.
    Sovereign of cities, seemliest in sight,
Of high renown, riches, and royalty;
    Of lords, barons, and many a goodly knight;
    Of most delectable lusty ladies bright;
Of famous prelates in habits clerical;
    Of merchants full of substance and might;
London, thou art the flower of cities all...

Above all rivers thy river hath renown,
    Whose beryl streams, pleasant and preclare,
Under thy lusty walls runneth down;
    Where many a swan doth swim with wings fair;
    Where many a barge doth sail, and row with oar,
Where many a ship doth rest with top-royal.
    O! town of towns, patron and not-compare:
London, thou art the flower of cities all...

Strong be thy walls that about thee stands;
    Wise be the people that within thee dwells;
Fresh is thy river with his lusty strands;
    Blithe be thy churches, well sounding be thy bells;
    Rich be thy merchants in substance that excels;
Fair be thy wives, right lovesome, white and small;
    Clear be thy virgins, lusty under kells:
London, thou art the flower of cities all.

(stanzas 1, 4 and 6)

WILLIAM DUNBAR (1465?–1530?)

Happiness

A state you must dare not enter
   with hopes of staying,
quicksand in the marshes, and all

the roads leading to a castle
   that doesn't exist.
But there it is, as promised,

with its perfect bridge above
   the crocodiles,
and its doors forever open.

STEPHEN DUNN (b. 1939)

from Ecclesiastes

What profit hath a man of all his labour which he taketh under
the sun?

One generation passeth away, and another generation cometh:
but the earth abideth for ever.

The sun also ariseth, and the sun goeth down, and hasteth to
his place where he arose.

The wind goeth toward the south, and turneth about unto the
north; it whirleth about continually, and the wind returneth
again according to his circuits.

All the rivers run into the sea; yet the sea is not full; unto the
place from whence the rivers come, thither they return
again.

THE KING JAMES BIBLE (1611)

Brooch

(*in memory of Stephanie Macleod*)

They have their place, accessories:
earrings, the odd necklace,
gemstone bracelets…

and yet, it's from the soft inner depth
we work the brooch of our lives,
that jewelled keepsake set to outlast us.

Yours, it was a brooch ablaze –
the passion-crafted clasp,
the light chain to keep it safe;

others, now, will wear your brooch –
this jewel fashioned from a golden heart.
It will catch the sun. It will dazzle us.

MENNA ELFYN (b. 1951)
translated from the Welsh by ELIN AP HYWEL

Prelude I

The winter evening settles down
With smell of steaks in passageways.
Six o'clock.
The burnt-out ends of smoky days.
And now a gusty shower wraps
The grimy scraps
Of withered leaves about your feet
And newspapers from vacant lots;
The showers beat
On broken blinds and chimney-pots,
And at the corner of the street
A lonely cab-horse steams and stamps.

And then the lighting of the lamps.

T.S. ELIOT (1888–1965)

Poem on the Underground

Proud readers
Hide behind tall newspapers.

The young are all arms and legs
Knackered by youth.

Tourists sit bolt upright
Trusting in nothing.

Only the drunk and the crazy
Aspire to converse.

Only the poet
Peruses his poem among the adverts.

Only the elderly person
Observes the request that the seat be offered to an
   elderly person.

D.J. ENRIGHT (1920–2002)

Optimistic Little Poem

Now and then it happens
that somebody shouts for help
and somebody else jumps in at once
and absolutely gratis.

Here in the thick of the grossest capitalism
round the corner comes the shining fire brigade
and extinguishes, or suddenly
there's silver in the beggar's hat.

Mornings the streets are full
of people hurrying here and there without
daggers in their hands, quite equably
after milk or radishes.

As though in a time of deepest peace.

A splendid sight.

HANS MAGNUS ENZENSBERGER (b. 1929)
translated by DAVID CONSTANTINE

A 14-Year-Old Convalescent Cat in the Winter

I want him to have another living summer,
to lie in the sun and enjoy the *douceur de vivre* –
because the sun, like golden rum in a rummer,
is what makes an idle cat *un tout petit peu ivre* –

I want him to lie stretched out, contented,
revelling in the heat, his fur all dry and warm,
an Old Age Pensioner, retired, resented
by no one, and happinesses in a beelike swarm

to settle on him – postponed for another season
that last fated hateful journey to the vet
from which there is no return (and age the reason),
which must soon come – as I cannot forget.

GAVIN EWART (1916–95)

Handbag

My mother's old leather handbag,
crowded with letters she carried
all through the war. The smell
of my mother's handbag: mints
and lipstick and Coty powder.
The look of those letters, softened
and worn at the edges, opened,
read, and refolded so often.
Letters from my father. Odour
of leather and powder, which ever
since then has meant womanliness,
and love, and anguish, and war.

RUTH FAINLIGHT (b. 1931)

Idyll

Not knowing even that we're on the way,
Until suddenly we're there. How shall we know?

There will be blackbirds, in a late March evening,
Blur of woodsmoke, whisky in grand glasses,

A poem of yours, waiting to be read; and one of mine;
A reflective bitch, a cat materialised

On a knee. All fears of present and future
Will be over, all guilts forgiven.

Maybe, heaven. Or maybe
We can get so far in this world. I'll believe we can.

U.A. FANTHORPE (1929–2009)

Monopoly

We sat like slum landlords around the board
buying each other out with fake banknotes,
until we lost more than we could afford,
or ever hope to pay back. Now our seats
are empty – one by one we left the game
to play for real, at first completely lost
in this other world, its building sites, its rain;
but slowly learned the rules or made our own,
stayed out of jail and kept our noses clean.
And now there's only me – sole freeholder
of every empty office space in town,
and from the quayside I can count the cost
each low tide brings – the skeletons and rust
of boats, cars, hats, boots, iron, a terrier.

PAUL FARLEY (b. 1965)

Wind

This is the wind, the wind in a field of corn.
Great crowds are fleeing from a major disaster
Down the long valleys, the green swaying wadis,
Down through the beautiful catastrophe of wind.

Families, tribes, nations and their livestock
Have heard something, seen something. An expectation
Or a gigantic misunderstanding has swept over the hilltop
Bending the ear of the hedgerow with stories of fire and sword.

I saw a thousand years pass in two seconds.
Land was lost, languages rose and divided.
This lord went east and found safety.
His brother sought Africa and a dish of aloes.

Centuries, minutes later, one might ask
How the hilt of a sword wandered so far from the smithy.
And somewhere they will sing: 'Like chaff we were borne
In the wind.' This is the wind in a field of corn.

JAMES FENTON (b. 1949)

'Fine Knacks for Ladies'

Fine knacks for ladies, cheap, choice, brave and new;
  Good pennyworths but money cannot move.
I keep a fair but for the fair to view.
  A beggar may be liberal of love;
Though all my wares be trash, the heart is true.

Great gifts are guiles and look for gifts again;
  My trifles come as treasures from my mind.
It is a precious jewel to be plain.
  Sometimes in shell the orient'st pearls we find;
Of others take a sheaf, of me a grain.

Within this pack pins, points, laces and gloves,
  And divers toys fitting a country fair;
But in my heart, where duty serves and loves,
  Turtles and twins, court's brood, a heavenly pair.
Happy the heart that thinks of no removes!

ANON. (before 1600)

Ballad of the Londoner

Evening falls on the smoky walls,
  And the railings drip with rain,
And I will cross the old river
  To see my girl again.

The great and solemn-gliding tram,
  Love's still-mysterious car,
Has many a light of gold and white,
  And a single dark red star.

I know a garden in a street
  Which no one ever knew;
I know a rose beyond the Thames,
  Where flowers are pale and few.

JAMES ELROY FLECKER (1884–1915)

The Visitor

In Spanish he whispers there is no time left.
It is the sound of scythes arcing in wheat,
the ache of some field song in Salvador.
The wind along the prison, cautious
as Francisco's hands on the inside, touching
the walls as he walks, it is his wife's breath
slipping into his cell each night while he
imagines his hand to be hers. It is a small country.

There is nothing one man will not do to another.

CAROLYN FORCHÉ (b. 1950)

A Collector

The things I found
But they'll scatter them again
to the four winds
as soon as I am dead

Old gadgets
fossilised plants and shells
books broken dolls
coloured postcards

And all the words
I have found
my incomplete
my unsatisfied words

ERICH FRIED (1921–88)
translated by STUART HOOD

Acquainted with the Night

I have been one acquainted with the night.
I have walked out in rain – and back in rain.
I have outwalked the furthest city light.

I have looked down the saddest city lane.
I have passed by the watchman on his beat
And dropped my eyes, unwilling to explain.

I have stood still and stopped the sound of feet
When far away an interrupted cry
Came over houses from another street,

But not to call me back or say good-by;
And further still at an unearthly height
One luminary clock against the sky

Proclaimed the time was neither wrong nor right.
I have been one acquainted with the night.

ROBERT FROST (1874–1963)

Concerto for Double Bass

He is a drunk leaning companionably
Around a lamp post or doing up
With intermittent concentration
Another drunk's coat.

He is a polite but devoted Valentino,
Cheek to cheek, forgetting the next step.
He is feeling the pulse of the fat lady
Or cutting her in half.

But close your eyes and it is sunset
At the edge of the world. It is the language
Of dolphins, the growth of tree-roots,
The heart-beat slowing down.

JOHN FULLER (b. 1937)

'The Great Frost'

O roving Muse, recall that wondrous year,
When winter reigned in bleak Britannia's air;
When hoary Thames, with frosted osiers crowned,
Was three long moons in icy fetters bound.
The waterman, forlorn along the shore,
Pensive reclines upon his useless oar,
Sees harnessed steeds desert the stony town,
And wander roads unstable, not their own;
Wheels o'er the hardened waters smoothly glide,
And rase with whitened tracks the slippery tide.
Here the fat cook piles high the blazing fire,
And scarce the spit can turn the steer entire.
Booths sudden hide the Thames, long streets appear,
And numerous games proclaim the crowded fair.

from TRIVIA,
OR THE ART OF WALKING THE STREETS OF LONDON

JOHN GAY (1685–1732)

The Undertaking

The darkness lifts, imagine, in your lifetime.
There you are – cased in clean bark you drift
through weaving rushes, fields flooded with cotton.
You are free. The river films with lilies,
shrubs appear, shoots thicken into palm. And now
all fear gives way: the light
looks after you, you feel the waves' goodwill
as arms widen over the water; Love,

the key is turned. Extend yourself –
it is the Nile, the sun is shining,
everywhere you turn is luck.

LOUISE GLÜCK (b. 1943)

I Am Becoming My Mother

Yellow/brown woman
fingers smelling always of onions

My mother raises rare blooms
and waters them with tea
her birth waters sang like rivers
my mother is now me

My mother had a linen dress
the colour of the sky
and stored lace and damask
tablecloths
to pull shame out of her eye.

I am becoming my mother
brown/yellow woman
fingers smelling always of onions.

LORNA GOODISON (b. 1947)

She Tells Her Love

She tells her love while half asleep,
  In the dark hours,
    With half-words whispered low:
As Earth stirs in her winter sleep
  And puts out grass and flowers
    Despite the snow,
    Despite the falling snow.

ROBERT GRAVES (1895–1985)

Love Without Hope

Love without hope, as when the young bird-catcher
Swept off his tall hat to the Squire's own daughter,
So let the imprisoned larks escape and fly
Singing about her head, as she rode by.

ROBERT GRAVES

'Gray goose and gander'

Gray goose and gander,
  Waft your wings together,
And carry the good king's daughter
  Over the one strand river.

ANON. (date unknown)

Sisu

To persevere in hope of summer.
To adapt to its broken promise.
To love winter.

To sleep.

To love winter.
To adapt to its broken promise.
To persevere in hope of summer.

LAVINIA GREENLAW (b. 1962)

Sisu: Finnish term for persevering in the face of adversity

The Reassurance

About ten days or so
After we saw you dead
You came back in a dream.
I'm all right now you said.

And it *was* you, although
You were fleshed out again:
You hugged us all round then,
And gave your welcoming beam.

How like you to be kind,
Seeking to reassure.
And, yes, how like my mind
To make itself secure.

THOM GUNN (1929–2004)

My children

I can hear them talking, my children
fluent English and broken Kurdish.

And whenever I disagree with them
they will comfort each other by saying:
Don't worry about mum, she's Kurdish.

Will I be the foreigner in my own home?

CHOMAN HARDI (b. 1974)

In Time of 'The Breaking of Nations'

I

Only a man harrowing clods
   In a slow silent walk
With an old horse that stumbles and nods
   Half asleep as they stalk.

II

Only thin smoke without flame
   From the heaps of couch-grass;
Yet this will go onward the same
   Though Dynasties pass.

III

Yonder a maid and her wight
   Come whispering by:
War's annals will cloud into night
   Ere their story die.

THOMAS HARDY (1840–1928)

'Thou art my battle axe and weapons of war: for with thee will I break in
pieces the nations, and with thee will I destroy kingdoms' (Jeremiah: 51.20).

Heredity

I am the family face;
Flesh perishes, I live on,
Projecting trait and trace
Through time to times anon,
And leaping from place to place
Over oblivion.

The years-heired feature that can
In curve and voice and eye
Despise the human span
Of durance – that is I;
The eternal thing in man,
That heeds no call to die.

THOMAS HARDY

The Railway Children

When we climbed the slopes of the cutting
We were eye-level with the white cups
Of the telegraph poles and the sizzling wires.

Like lovely freehand they curved for miles
East and miles west beyond us, sagging
Under their burden of swallows.

We were small and thought we knew nothing
Worth knowing. We thought words travelled the wires
In the shiny pouches of raindrops,

Each one seeded full with the light
Of the sky, the gleam of the lines, and ourselves
So infinitesimally scaled

We could stream through the eye of a needle.

SEAMUS HEANEY (b. 1939)

The Rescue

In drifts of sleep I came upon you
Buried to your waist in snow.
You reached your arms out: I came to
Like water in a dream of thaw.

SEAMUS HEANEY

The Unpredicted

The goddess Fortune be praised (on her toothed wheel
I have been mincemeat these several years)
Last night, for a whole night, the unpredictable
Lay in my arms, in a tender and unquiet rest –
(I perceived the irrelevance of my former tears) –
Lay, and at dawn departed. I rose and walked the streets
Where a whitsuntide wind blew fresh, and blackbirds
Incontestably sang, and the people were beautiful.

JOHN HEATH-STUBBS (1918–2006)

Into Rail

The first train I rode in I rode in when I was eight
it was a beautiful beast, a great
one-nostrilled, black dragon
cheerfully dragging its human wagon loads.
Now the nostrils have gone
but the benevolence goes on.
The loco lives
the loco gives.
Even the trains
I do not catch
transport me.

JOHN HEGLEY (b. 1953)

Everything Changes

after Brecht, *'Alles wandelt sich'*

Everything changes. We plant
trees for those born later
but what's happened has happened,
and poisons poured into the seas
cannot be drained out again.

What's happened has happened.
Poisons poured into the seas
cannot be drained out again, but
everything changes. We plant
trees for those born later.

CICELY HERBERT (b. 1937)

Virtue

Sweet day, so cool, so calm, so bright,
The bridal of the earth and sky:
The dew shall weep thy fall tonight;
                    For thou must die.

Sweet rose, whose hue angry and brave
Bids the rash gazer wipe his eye:
Thy root is ever in its grave,
                    And thou must die.

Sweet spring, full of sweet days and roses,
A box where sweets compacted lie;
My music shows ye have your closes,
                    And all must die.

Only a sweet and virtuous soul,
Like seasoned timber, never gives;
But though the whole world turn to coal,
                    Then chiefly lives.

GEORGE HERBERT (1593–1633)

The Argument of His Book

I sing of Brooks, of Blossomes, Birds, and Bowers:
Of April, May, of June, and July-Flowers.
I sing of May-poles, Hock-carts, Wassails, Wakes,
Of Bride-grooms, Brides, and of their Bridall-cakes.
I write of Youth, of Love, and have Accesse
By these, to sing of cleanly-Wantonnesse.
I sing of Dewes, of Raines, and piece by piece
Of Balme, of Oyle, of Spice, and Amber-Greece.
I sing of Times trans-shifting; and I write
How Roses first came Red, and Lillies White.
I write of Groves, of Twilights, and I sing
The Court of Mab, and of the Fairie-King.
I write of Hell; I sing (and ever shall)
Of Heaven, and hope to have it after all.

ROBERT HERRICK (1591–1674)

Dreams

Here we are all, by day; by night we're hurled
By dreams, each one, into a several world.

ROBERT HERRICK

Merlin

I will consider the outnumbering dead:
For they are the husks of what was rich seed.
Now, should they come together to be fed,
They would outstrip the locusts' covering tide.

Arthur, Elaine, Mordred; they are all gone
Among the raftered galleries of bone.
By the long barrows of Logres they are made one,
And over their city stands the pinnacled corn.

GEOFFREY HILL (b. 1932)

Spacetime

When I grow up and you get small,
then –

(In Kaluza's theory the fifth dimension
is represented as a circle
associated with every point
in spacetime)

– then when I die, I'll never be alive again?
           Never.
Never never?
           Never never.
Yes, but never never never?
             No . . . not never never never,
             just never never.

So we made
a small family contribution
to the quantum problem of eleven-dimensional
   supergravity.

MIROSLAV HOLUB (1923–98)
translated by DAVID YOUNG *and* DANA HÁBOVÁ

The Gateway

Now the heart sings with all its thousand voices
To hear this city of cells, my body, sing.
The tree through the stiff clay at long last forces
Its thin strong roots and taps the secret spring.

And the sweet waters without intermission
Climb to the tips of its green tenement;
The breasts have borne the grace of their possession,
The lips have felt the pressure of content.

Here I come home: in this expected country
They know my name and speak it with delight.
I am the dream and you my gates of entry,
The means by which I waken into light.

A.D. HOPE (1907–2000)

Inversnaid

This dárksome búrn, hórseback brówn,
His rollrock highroad roaring down,
In coop and in comb the fleece of his foam
Flutes and low to the lake falls home.

A windpuff-bónnet of fáwn-fróth
Turns and twindles over the broth
Of a pool so pitchblack, féll-frówning,
It rounds and rounds Despair to drowning.

Degged with dew, dappled with dew
Are the groins of the braes that the brook treads through,
Wiry heathpacks, flitches of fern,
And the beadbonny ash that sits over the burn.

What would the world be, once bereft
Of wet and of wildness? Let them be left,
O let them be left, wildness and wet;
Long live the weeds and the wilderness yet.

GERARD MANLEY HOPKINS (1844–89)

'Into my heart an air that kills'

Into my heart an air that kills
   From yon far country blows:
What are those blue remembered hills,
   What spires, what farms are those?

That is the land of lost content,
   I see it shining plain,
The happy highways where I went
   And cannot come again.

A.E. HOUSMAN (1859–1936)

'When I was one-and-twenty'

When I was one-and-twenty
   I heard a wise man say,
'Give crowns and pounds and guineas
   But not your heart away;
Give pearls away and rubies
   But keep your fancy free.'
But I was one-and-twenty,
   No use to talk to me.

When I was one-and-twenty
   I heard him say again,
'The heart out of the bosom
   Was never given in vain;
'Tis paid with sighs a plenty
   And sold for endless rue.'
And I am two-and-twenty,
   And oh, 'tis true, 'tis true.

A.E. HOUSMAN

Dream Boogie

Good morning, daddy!
Ain't you heard
The boogie-woogie rumble
Of a dream deferred?

Listen closely:
You'll hear their feet
Beating out and beating out a –

> *You think*
> *It's a happy beat?*

Listen to it closely:
Ain't you heard
something underneath
like a —

> *What did I say?*

Sure,
I'm happy!
Take it away!

> *Hey, pop!*
> *Re-bop!*
> *Mop!*

> *Y-e-a-h!*

LANGSTON HUGHES (1902–67)

Full Moon and Little Frieda

A cool small evening shrunk to a dog bark and the clank
                                        of a bucket –

And you listening.
A spider's web, tense for the dew's touch.
A pail lifted, still and brimming – mirror
To tempt a first star to a tremor.

Cows are going home in the lane there, looping the hedges
                        with their warm wreaths of breath –
A dark river of blood, many boulders,
Balancing unspilled milk.

'Moon!' you cry suddenly, 'Moon! Moon!'

The moon has stepped back like an artist gazing amazed
                                        at a work
That points at him amazed.

TED HUGHES (1930–98)

The Embankment

*(The Fantasia of a Fallen Gentleman on a
Cold, Bitter Night)*

Once, in finesse of fiddles found I ecstasy,
In a flash of gold heels on the hard pavement.
Now see I
That warmth's the very stuff of poesy.
Oh, God, make small
The old star-eaten blanket of the sky,
That I may fold it round me and in comfort lie.

T.E. HULME (1883–1917)

'I have a gentil cock'

I have a gentil cock
croweth me day
he doth me risen early
my matins for to say

I have a gentil cock
comen he is of great
his comb is of red coral
his tail is of jet

I have a gentil cock
comen he is of kind
his comb is of red sorrel
his tail is of inde

his legs be of azure
so gentil and so small
his spurs are of silver white
into the wortewale

his eyes are of crystal
locked all in amber
and every night he percheth him
in my lady's chamber

ANON. (early 15th century)

'I sing of a maiden'

I sing of a maiden
that is makeles
King of all kings
to her son she chose

he came also still
there his mother was
as dew in April
that falleth on the grass

he came also still
to his mother's bower
as dew in April
that falleth on the flower

he came also still
there his mother lay
as dew in April
that falleth on the spray

mother and maiden
was never none but she
well may such a lady
God's mother be

ANON. (early 15th century)

makeles: matchless

'I have a young sister'

I have a young sister far beyond the sea
many be the druries that she sent me

she sent me the cherry without any stone
and so she did the dove without any bone

she sent me the briar without any rind
she bade me love my leman without longing

how should any cherry be without stone
and how should any dove be without bone

how should any briar be without rind
how should any love my leman without longing

when the cherry was a flower then had it no stone
when the dove was an egg then had it no bone

when the briar was unbred then had it no rind
when the maiden hath that she loveth she is without longing

ANON. (early 15th century)

druries: love-gifts   *leman:* sweetheart   *unbred:* unborn

I shall say what inordinate love is:
The furiosity and wodness of mind,
An instinguible burning, faulting bliss,
A great hunger, insatiate to find,
A dulcet ill, an evil sweetness blind,
A right wonderful sugared sweet error,
Without labour rest, contrary to kind,
Or without quiet, to have huge labour.

ANON. (15th century)

wodness: frenzy

'I saw a Peacock with a fiery tail'

I saw a Peacock with a fiery tail
I saw a blazing Comet drop down hail
I saw a Cloud with Ivy circled round
I saw a sturdy Oak creep on the ground
I saw a Pismire swallow up a Whale
I saw a raging Sea brim full of Ale
I saw a Venice Glass sixteen foot deep
I saw a Well full of men's tears that weep
I saw their Eyes all in a flame of fire
I saw a House as big as the Moon and higher
I saw the Sun even in the midst of night
I saw the Man that saw this wondrous sight.

ANON. (17th century)

N.W.2: Spring

The poets never lied when they praised
Spring in England.
                        Even in this neat suburb
You can feel there's something to
                                their pastorals.
Something gentle, broadly nostalgic, is stirring
On the well-aired pavements.
                        Indrawn brick
Sighs, and you notice the sudden sharpness
Of things growing.
                        The sun lightens
The significance of what the houses
Are steeped in,
                brightens out
Their winter brooding.
                        Early May
Touches also the cold diasporas
That England hardly mentions.

A.C. JACOBS (1937–94)

Distances

Swifts turn in the heights of the air;
higher still turn the invisible stars.
When day withdraws to the ends of the earth
their fires shine on a dark expanse of sand.

We live in a world of motion and distance.
The heart flies from tree to bird,
from bird to distant star,
from star to love; and love grows
in the quiet house, turning and working,
servant of thought, a lamp held in one hand.

PHILIPPE JACCOTTET (b. 1925)
translated by DEREK MAHON

Rooms

Though I love this travelling life and yearn
like ships docked, I long
for rooms to open with my bare hands,
and there discover the wonderful, say
a ship's prow rearing, and a ladder
of rope thrown down.
Though young, I'm weary:
I'm all rooms at present, all doors
fastened against me;
but once admitted start craving
and swell for a fine, listing ocean-going prow
no man in creation can build me.

KATHLEEN JAMIE (b. 1962)

The Creel

The world began with a woman,
shawl-happed, stooped under a creel,
whose slow step you recognize
from troubled dreams. You feel

obliged to help bear her burden
from hill or kelp-strewn shore,
but she passes by unseeing
thirled to her private chore.

It's not sea birds or peat she's carrying,
not fleece, nor the herring bright
but her fear that if ever she put it down
the world would go out like a light.

KATHLEEN JAMIE

creel: wicker basket for carrying fish, peat, etc. on the back
thirled: enslaved

Delay

The radiance of that star that leans on me
Was shining years ago. The light that now
Glitters up there my eye may never see,
And so the time lag teases me with how

Love that loves now may not reach me until
Its first desire is spent. The star's impulse
Must wait for eyes to claim it beautiful
And love arrived may find us somewhere else.

ELIZABETH JENNINGS (1926–2001)

Bonnard

Colour of rooms. Pastel shades. Crowds. Torsos at ease in
brilliant baths. And always, everywhere the light.

This is a way of creating the world again, of seeing
differences, of piling shadow on shadow, of showing up
distances, of bringing close, bringing close.

A way of furnishing too, of making yourself feel at home –
and others. Pink, flame, coral, yellow, magenta – extreme
colours for ordinary situations. This is a way to make a
new world.

Then watch it. Let the colours dry, let the carpets collect
a little dust. Let the walls peel gently, and people come,
innocent, nude, eager for bed or bath.

They look newmade too, these bodies, newborn and
innocent. Their flesh-tints fit the bright walls and floors
and they take a bath as if entering the first stream, the
first fountain.

ELIZABETH JENNINGS

Song

to Celia

Drink to me only with thine eyes,
  And I will pledge with mine;
Or leave a kiss but in the cup,
  And I'll not look for wine.
The thirst that from the soul doth rise
  Doth ask a drink divine;
But might I of Jove's nectar sup,
  I would not change for thine.

I sent thee late a rosy wreath,
  Not so much honouring thee
As giving it a hope that there
  It could not withered be.
But thou thereon didst only breathe,
  And sent'st it back to me;
Since when it grows, and smells, I swear,
  Not of itself, but thee.

BEN JONSON (1572–1637)

Tides

There are some coasts
Where the sea comes in spectacularly
Throwing itself up gullies, challenging cliffs,
Filling the harbours with great swirls and flourish,
A theatrical event that people gather for
Curtain up twice daily. You need to know
The hour of its starting, you have to be on guard.

There are other places
Places where you do not really notice
The gradual stretch of the fertile silk of water
No gurgling or dashings here, no froth no pounding
Only at some point the echo may sound different
And looking by chance one sees 'Oh the tide is in.'

JENNY JOSEPH (b. 1932)

Wet Evening in April

The birds sang in the wet trees
And as I listened to them it was a hundred years from now
And I was dead and someone else was listening to them.
But I was glad I had recorded for him
   The melancholy.

PATRICK KAVANAGH (1906–67)

Memory of My Father

Every old man I see
Reminds me of my father
When he had fallen in love with death
One time when sheaves were gathered.

That man I saw in Gardner Street
Stumble on the kerb was one,
He stared at me half-eyed,
I might have been his son.

And I remember the musician
Faltering over his fiddle
In Bayswater, London,
He too set me the riddle.

Every old man I see
In October-coloured weather
Seems to say to me:
'I was once your father.'

PATRICK KAVANAGH

Promise

Remember, the time of year
when the future appears
like a blank sheet of paper
a clean calendar, a new chance.
On thick white snow

you vow fresh footprints
then watch them go
with the wind's hearty gust.
Fill your glass. Here's tae us. Promises
made to be broken, made to last.

JACKIE KAY (b. 1961)

Freight song

We were lying, the two of us
on a freight lift platform

which four angels were hoisting up,
their haloes journeying

little by little up to blue sky.
And you were stacked next to me

and I was stacked alongside you
like two symbiotic suitcases

with labels reading: The Twilit Sky.
Our sleepy lift attendants

were the stars of heaven.
And we were the goods –

JUDITH KAZANTZIS (b. 1940)

On First Looking into Chapman's Homer

Much have I travell'd in the realms of gold,
 And many goodly states and kingdoms seen;
 Round many western islands have I been
Which bards in fealty to Apollo hold.
Oft of one wide expanse had I been told
 That deep-brow'd Homer ruled as his demesne;
 Yet did I never breathe its pure serene
Till I heard Chapman speak out loud and bold:
Then felt I like some watcher of the skies
 When a new planet swims into his ken;
Or like stout Cortez when with eagle eyes
 He star'd at the Pacific – and all his men
Look'd at each other with a wild surmise –
 Silent, upon a peak in Darien.

JOHN KEATS (1795–1821)

When I have fears that I may cease to be
   Before my pen has glean'd my teeming brain,
Before high-pilèd books, in charact'ry,
   Hold like rich garners the full-ripen'd grain;
When I behold, upon the night's starr'd face,
   Huge cloudy symbols of a high romance,
And think that I may never live to trace
   Their shadows, with the magic hand of chance;
And when I feel, fair creature of an hour!
   That I shall never look upon thee more,
Never have relish in the faery power
   Of unreflecting love! – then on the shore
Of the wide world I stand alone, and think
Till love and fame to nothingness do sink.

JOHN KEATS

To Someone Who Insisted I Look Up Someone

I rang them up while touring Timbuctoo,
Those bosom chums to whom you're known as *'Who?'*

X.J. KENNEDY (b. 1929)

Thanks Forever

Look at those empty ships
floating north
between south-running ice
like big tulips
in the Narrows
under the Verrazano
toward the city harbor.
I'm parked here,
out of work all year.
No hurry now
and sleep badly.
But I'm self-employed.
My new job's
to wave them in.
Hello freighter,
hello tanker.
Welcome, welcome,
to New York.

MILTON KESSLER (1930–2000)

Apology

Humming your Nocturne on the Circle Line,
unlike the piano, running out of breath

I've been writing you out of my life
my loves (one out, one in).

I've pushed you out of the way to see
what the gaps in my life might look like,

how large they are,
how quickly I could write them in;

and not (at least till I've lost you both)
rewriting you only means

that the spaces I'm not writing in are where
I live.

MIMI KHALVATI (b. 1944)

Sic Vita

Like to the falling of a star;
Or as the flights of eagles are;
Or like the fresh spring's gaudy hue;
Or silver drops of morning dew;
Or like a wind that chafes the flood;
Or bubbles which on water stood;
Even such is man, whose borrowed light
Is straight called in, and paid to night.

The wind blows out; the bubble dies;
The spring entombed in autumn lies;
The dew dries up; the star is shot;
The flight is past; and man forgot.

HENRY KING (1592–1669)

from The Vision of Piers Plowman

'After sharp showers,' said Peace, 'the sun shines brightest;
No weather is warmer than after watery clouds;
Nor any love dearer, or more loving friends,
Than after war and woe, when Love and Peace are masters.
There was never war in this world, or wickedness so keen,
That Love, if he liked, could not turn to laughter,
And Peace, through patience, put an end to all perils.'

(Passus 18, lines 413–17)

WILLIAM LANGLAND (*c.* 1332–1400)

A Dead Statesman

I could not dig: I dared not rob:
Therefore I lied to please the mob.
Now all my lies are proved untrue
And I must face the men I slew.
What tale shall serve me here among
Mine angry and defrauded young?

from EPITAPHS OF THE WAR 1914–18

RUDYARD KIPLING (1865–1936)

Voyage to the Bottom of the Sea

The trick (he tells me) is to sleep till twelve
    then watch the television.
In the corner of his murky bedroom
    there is always a swirl of colour:

T-shirts; smoke threading from an ashtray
    to the light; shoes; anemones thriving
on the wreck of the Torrey Canyon;
    our Chancellor raising the Budget box.

STEPHEN KNIGHT (b. 1960)

Exodus

For all mothers in anguish
Pushing out their babies
In a small basket

To let the river cradle them
And kind hands find
And nurture them

Providing safety
In a hostile world:
Our constant gratitude.

As in this last century
The crowded trains
Taking us away from home

Became our baby baskets
Rattling to foreign parts
Our exodus from death.

LOTTE KRAMER (b. 1923)

The Trees

The trees are coming into leaf
Like something almost being said;
The recent buds relax and spread,
Their greenness is a kind of grief.

Is it that they are born again
And we grow old? No, they die too.
Their yearly trick of looking new
Is written down in rings of grain.

Yet still the unresting castles thresh
In fullgrown thickness every May.
Last year is dead, they seem to say,
Begin afresh, afresh, afresh.

PHILIP LARKIN (1922–85)

Cut Grass

Cut grass lies frail:
Brief is the breath
Mown stalks exhale.
Long, long the death

It dies in the white hours
Of young-leafed June
With chestnut flowers,
With hedges snowlike strewn,

White lilac bowed,
Lost lanes of Queen Anne's lace,
And that high-builded cloud
Moving at summer's pace.

PHILIP LARKIN

Piano

Softly, in the dusk, a woman is singing to me;
Taking me back down the vista of years, till I see
A child sitting under the piano, in the boom of the tingling
    strings
And pressing the small, poised feet of a mother who smiles
    as she sings.

In spite of myself, the insidious mastery of song
Betrays me back, till the heart of me weeps to belong
To the old Sunday evenings at home, with winter outside
And hymns in the cosy parlour, the tinkling piano our guide.

So now it is vain for the singer to burst into clamour
With the great black piano appassionato. The glamour
Of childish days is upon me, my manhood is cast
Down in the flood of remembrance, I weep like a child for
    the past.

D.H. LAWRENCE (1885–1930)

There was an Old Man with a beard,
Who said, 'It is just as I feared! –
   Two Owls and a Hen,
   Four Larks and a Wren,
Have all built their nests in my beard!'

EDWARD LEAR (1812–88)

'There was an Old Man with a beard' Drawing by the author, from
The Book of Nonsense.

The Long War

Less passionate the long war throws
its burning thorn about all men,
caught in one grief, we share one wound,
and cry one dialect of pain.

We have forgot who fired the house,
whose easy mischief spilt first blood,
under one raging roof we lie
the fault no longer understood.

But as our twisted arms embrace
the desert where our cities stood,
death's family likeness in each face
must show, at last, our brotherhood.

LAURIE LEE (1914–97)

Living

The fire in leaf and grass
so green it seems
each summer the last summer.

The wind blowing, the leaves
shivering in the sun,
each day the last day.

A red salamander
so cold and so
easy to catch, dreamily

moves his delicate feet
and long tail. I hold
my hand open for him to go.

Each minute the last minute.

DENISE LEVERTOV (1923–97)

Industrial

From a bridge, the inverted *vanitas*
Of a swan drifting down a black canal
Between two corrugated warehouses.

FRANCES LEVISTON (b. 1982)

Listening to a Monk from Shu
Playing the Lute

The monk from Shu with his green lute-case walked
Westward down Emei Shan, and at the sound
Of the first notes he strummed for me I heard
A thousand valleys' rustling pines resound.
My heart was cleansed, as if in flowing water.
In bells of frost I heard the resonance die.
Dusk came unnoticed over the emerald hills
And autumn clouds layered the darkening sky.

LI BAI (AD 701–61)
translated by VIKRAM SETH

Calligraphy by Qu Lei Lei

London Airport

Last night in London Airport
I saw a wooden bin
labelled UNWANTED LITERATURE
IS TO BE PLACED HEREIN.
So I wrote a poem
and popped it in.

CHRISTOPHER LOGUE (b. 1926)

Greenwich Park

Spring's come, a little late, in the park:
a tree-rat smokes flat 'S's over the lawn.
A mallard has somehow forgotten something
it can't quite remember. Daffodils yawn,
prick their ears, push their muzzles out
for a kiss. Pansies spoof pensive
Priapus faces: Socrates or Verlaine.
A cock-pigeon is sexually harassing
a hen: pecking and poking and padding
behind her impertinently, bowing and mowing.
But when he's suddenly absent-minded –
can't keep even sex in his head –
she trembles, stops her gadding, doubts
and grazes his way. He remembers and pouts.

HERBERT LOMAS (b. 1924)

London Bells

Two sticks and an apple,
Ring the bells at Whitechapel.

Old Father Bald Pate,
Ring the bells at Aldgate.

Maids in white aprons,
Ring the bells at St. Catherine's.

Oranges and lemons,
Ring the bells at St. Clement's.

When will you pay me?
Ring the bells at the Old Bailey.

When I am rich,
Ring the bells at Fleetditch.

When will that be?
Ring the bells at Stepney.

When I am old,
Ring the great bell at Paul's.

ANON. (early 18th century)

The Sunburst

Her first memory is of light all around her
As she sits among pillows on a patchwork quilt
Made out of uniforms, coat linings, petticoats,
Waistcoats, flannel shirts, ball gowns, by Mother
Or Grandmother, twenty stitches to every inch,
A flawless version of *World without End* or
Cathedral Window or a diamond pattern
That radiates from the smallest grey square
Until the sunburst fades into the calico.

MICHAEL LONGLEY (b. 1939)

To Althea, from Prison

When Love with unconfinèd wings
  Hovers within my gates,
And my divine Althea brings
  To whisper at the grates;
When I lie tangled in her hair
  And fettered to her eye,
The gods that wanton in the air
  Know no such liberty...

Stone walls do not a prison make,
  Nor iron bars a cage;
Minds innocent and quiet take
  That for an hermitage.
If I have freedom in my love,
  And in my soul am free,
Angels alone, that soar above,
  Enjoy such liberty.

RICHARD LOVELACE (1618–57)

Stars and planets

Trees are cages for them: water holds its breath
To balance them without smudging on its delicate meniscus.
Children watch them playing in their heavenly playground;
Men use them to lug ships across oceans, through firths.

They seem so twinkle-still, but they never cease
Inventing new spaces and huge explosions
And migrating in mathematical tribes over
The steppes of space at their outrageous ease.

It's hard to think that the earth is one –
This poor sad bearer of wars and disasters
Rolls-Roycing round the sun with its load of gangsters,
Attended only by the loveless moon.

NORMAN MacCAIG (1910–96)

February – not everywhere

Such days, when trees run downwind,
their arms stretched before them.

Such days, when the sun's in a drawer
and the drawer locked.

When the meadow is dead, is a carpet,
thin and shabby, with no pattern

and at bus stops people retract into collars
their faces like fists.

– And when, in a firelit room, a mother looks
at her four seasons, at her little boy,

in the centre of everything, with still pools
of shadows and a fire throwing flowers.

NORMAN MacCAIG

The Bonnie Broukit Bairn

Mars is braw in crammasy,
Venus in a green silk goun,
The auld mune shak's her gowden feathers,
Their starry talk's a wheen o' blethers,
Nane for thee a thochtie sparin',
Earth, thou bonnie broukit bairn!
– But greet, an' in your tears ye'll drown
The haill clanjamfrie!

HUGH MacDIARMID (CHRISTOPHER MURRAY GRIEVE)
(1892–1978)

braw: fine   *crammasy:* crimson   *a wheen o' blethers:* a pack of nonsense
broukit: neglected   *greet:* weep   *the haill clanjamfrie:* the whole caboodle

The Leader

I wanna be the leader
I wanna be the leader
Can I be the leader?
Can I? I can?
Promise? Promise?
Yippee, I'm the leader
I'm the leader

OK what shall we do?

ROGER McGOUGH (b. 1937)

Words in Time

Bewildered with the broken tongue
Of wakened angels in our sleep –
Then, lost the music that was sung
And lost the light time cannot keep!

There is a moment when we lie
Bewildered, wakened out of sleep,
When light and sound and all reply:
That moment time must tame and keep.

That moment, like a flight of birds
Flung from the branches where they sleep,
The poet with a beat of words
Flings into time for time to keep.

ARCHIBALD MacLEISH (1892–1982)

Snow

The room was suddenly rich and the great bay-window was
Spawning snow and pink roses against it
Soundlessly collateral and incompatible:
World is suddener than we fancy it.

World is crazier and more of it than we think,
Incorrigibly plural. I peel and portion
A tangerine and spit the pips and feel
The drunkenness of things being various.

And the fire flames with a bubbling sound for world
Is more spiteful and gay than one supposes –
On the tongue on the eyes on the ears in the palms of one's
    hands –
There is more than glass between the snow and the huge
    roses.

LOUIS MacNEICE (1907–63)

Coda

Maybe we knew each other better
When the night was young and unrepeated
And the moon stood still over Jericho.

So much for the past; in the present
There are moments caught between heart-beats
When maybe we know each other better.

But what is that clinking in the darkness?
Maybe we shall know each other better
When the tunnels meet beneath the mountain.

LOUIS MacNEICE

'When you stop to consider
The days spent dreaming of a future
And say then, that was my life.'

For the days are long –
From the first milk van
To the last shout in the night,
An eternity. But the weeks go by
Like birds; and the years, the years
Fly past anti-clockwise
Like clock hands in a bar mirror.

DEREK MAHON (b. 1941)

The Maiden's Song

When I was in my mother's bower
I had all that I would

The bailey beareth the bell away
The lily, the rose, the rose I lay

The silver is white, red is the gold
The robes they lay in fold

The bailey beareth the bell away
The lily, the rose, the rose I lay

And through the glass window shines the sun
How should I love and I so young

The bailey beareth the bell away
The lily, the rose, the rose I lay
The bailey beareth the bell away

ANON. (16th century)

Thaw

The season midnight: glass
cracks with cold. From lighted shop-windows

girls half-sleeping, numb with frost step out.
We warm their hands between our hands, we kiss them

awake, and the planets
melt on their cheeks.

First touch, first tears. Behind their blue eyes darkness
shatters its pane of ice. We

step through into a forest
of sunlight, sunflowers.

DAVID MALOUF (b. 1934)

'You took away all the oceans and all the room'

You took away all the oceans and all the room.
You gave me my shoe-size in earth with bars around it.
Where did it get you? Nowhere.
You left me my lips, and they shape words, even in silence.

OSIP MANDELSTAM (1891–1938)
translated by CLARENCE BROWN *and* W.S. MERWIN

The Thing Not Said

We need life-jackets now to float
On words which leave so much unsaid.

How can this not sound like sophistry
To justify absence from your thoughts, your bed?

But this haemorrhaging of language
Still keeps the best phrase locked in my head.

Easy to talk of loneliness, of ageing, damning
Those who would be Presidents and Generals of the dead;

Forgetting the detail, the particular hunger
Of someone you know waiting to be fed.

And now I'm doing it again, drifting on words,
More lines for the simple thing not said.

E.A. MARKHAM (1939–2008)

The Passionate Shepherd to his Love

Come live with me, and be my love,
And we will all the pleasures prove
That valleys, groves, hills and fields,
Woods, or steepy mountain yields.

And we will sit upon the rocks,
Seeing the shepherds feed their flocks
By shallow rivers, to whose falls
Melodious birds sing madrigals.

And I will make thee beds of roses,
And a thousand fragrant posies,
A cap of flowers, and a kirtle,
Embroidered all with leaves of myrtle.

A gown made of the finest wool
Which from our pretty lambs we pull,
Fair lined slippers for the cold,
With buckles of the purest gold.

A belt of straw and ivy buds,
With coral clasps and amber studs,
And if these pleasures may thee move,
Come live with me, and be my love.

The shepherd swains shall dance and sing
For thy delight each May-morning;
If these delights thy mind may move,
Then live with me, and be my love.

CHRISTOPHER MARLOWE (1564–93)

Cargoes

Quinquireme of Nineveh from distant Ophir
Rowing home to haven in sunny Palestine,
With a cargo of ivory,
And apes and peacocks,
Sandalwood, cedarwood, and sweet white wine.

Stately Spanish galleon coming from the Isthmus,
Dipping through the Tropics by the palm-green shores,
With a cargo of diamonds,
Emeralds, amethysts,
Topazes, and cinnamon, and gold moidores.

Dirty British coaster with a salt-caked smoke stack
Butting through the Channel in the mad March days,
With a cargo of Tyne coal,
Road-rails, pig-lead,
Firewood, iron-ware, and cheap tin trays.

JOHN MASEFIELD (1878–1967)

Listening to a Monk from Shu
Playing the Lute

The monk from Shu with his green lute-case walked
Westward down Emei Shan, and at the sound
Of the first notes he strummed for me I heard
A thousand valleys' rustling pines resound.
My heart was cleansed, as if in flowing water.
In bells of frost I heard the resonance die.
Dusk came unnoticed over the emerald hills
And autumn clouds layered the darkening sky.

LI BAI (AD 701–61)

translated by VIKRAM SETH

Calligraphy by Qu Lei Lei

Separation

Your absence has gone through me
Like thread through a needle.
Everything I do is stitched with its colour.

W.S. MERWIN (b. 1927)

Rain Travel

I wake in the dark and remember
it is the morning when I must start
by myself on the journey
I lie listening to the black hour
before dawn and you are
still asleep beside me while
around us the trees full of night lean
hushed in their dream that bears
us up asleep and awake then I hear
drops falling one by one into
the sightless leaves and I
do not know when they began but
all at once there is no sound but rain
and the stream below us roaring
away into the rushing darkness

W.S. MERWIN

Sea Love

Tide be runnin' the great world over:
    'Twas only last June month I mind that we
Was thinkin' the toss and the call in the breast of the lover
    So everlastin' as the sea.

Heer's the same little fishes that sputter and swim,
    Wi' the moon's old glim on the grey, wet sand;
An' him no more to me nor me to him
    Than the wind goin' over my hand.

CHARLOTTE MEW (1869–1928)

'What lips my lips have kissed'

What lips my lips have kissed, and where, and why,
I have forgotten, and what arms have lain
Under my head till morning; but the rain
Is full of ghosts tonight, that tap and sigh
Upon the glass and listen for reply,
And in my heart there stirs a quiet pain
For unremembered lads that not again
Will turn to me at midnight with a cry.
Thus in the winter stands the lonely tree,
Nor knows what birds have vanished one by one,
Yet knows its boughs more silent than before:
I cannot say what loves have come and gone,
I only know that summer sang in me
A little while, that in me sings no more.

EDNA ST. VINCENT MILLAY (1892–1950)

Teeth

English Teeth, English Teeth!
Shining in the sun
A part of British heritage
Aye, each and every one.

English Teeth, Happy Teeth!
Always having fun
Clamping down on bits of fish
And sausages half done.

English Teeth! HEROES' Teeth!
Hear them click! and clack!
Let's sing a song of praise to them –
Three Cheers for the Brown Grey and Black.

SPIKE MILLIGAN (1918–2002)

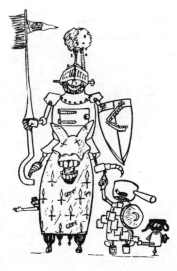

Teeth   Drawing by the
author, in *Silly Verse for Kids*
© Spike Milligan, by permission
of Spike Milligan Productions.

And Yet the Books

And yet the books will be there on the shelves, separate beings,
That appeared once, still wet
As shining chestnuts under a tree in autumn,
And, touched, coddled, began to live
In spite of fires on the horizon, castles blown up,
Tribes on the march, planets in motion.
'We are,' they said, even as their pages
Were being torn out, or a buzzing flame
Licked away their letters. So much more durable
Than we are, whose frail warmth
Cools down with memory, disperses, perishes.
I imagine the earth when I am no more:
Nothing happens, no loss, it's still a strange pageant,
Women's dresses, dewy lilacs, a song in the valley.
Yet the books will be there on the shelves, well born,
Derived from people, but also from radiance, heights.

CZESLAW MILOSZ (1911–2004)

translated by CZESLAW MILOSZ *and* ROBERT HASS

Sonnet: On His Blindness

When I consider how my light is spent,
   Ere half my days, in this dark world and wide,
   And that one talent which is death to hide,
   Lodged with me useless, though my soul more bent
To serve therewith my maker, and present
   My true account, lest he returning chide,
   Doth God exact day-labour, light denied?
   I fondly ask; but Patience to prevent
That murmur, soon replies, God doth not need
   Either man's work or his own gifts, who best
   Bear his mild yoke, they serve him best, his state
Is kingly. Thousands at his bidding speed
   And post o'er land and ocean without rest:
   They also serve who only stand and wait.

JOHN MILTON (1608–74)

Song: On May Morning

Now the bright morning star, day's harbinger,
Comes dancing from the east, and leads with her
The flowery May, who from her green lap throws
The yellow cowslip, and the pale primrose.
    Hail bounteous May that dost inspire
    Mirth and youth and warm desire!
    Woods and groves are of thy dressing,
    Hill and dale doth boast thy blessing.
Thus we salute thee with our early song,
And welcome thee, and wish thee long.

JOHN MILTON

Song *from* Comus

Attendant Spirit: Sabrina fair
  Listen where thou art sitting
Under the glassy, cool, translucent wave,
  In twisted braids of lilies knitting
The loose train of thy amber-dropping hair;
  Listen for dear honour's sake,
  Goddess of the silver lake,
    Listen and save.

Sabrina: By the rushy-fringed bank,
Where grows the willow and the osier dank,
  My sliding chariot stays,
Thick set with agate, and the azurn sheen
Of turquoise blue, and emerald green
  That in the channel strays,
Whilst from off the waters fleet
Thus I set my printless feet
O'er the cowslip's velvet head,
  That bends not as I tread,
Gentle swain at thy request
    I am here.

JOHN MILTON

Celia Celia

When I am sad and weary
When I think all hope has gone
When I walk along High Holborn
I think of you with nothing on

ADRIAN MITCHELL (1932–2008)

Goodbye

He breathed in air, he breathed out light.
Charlie Parker was my delight.

ADRIAN MITCHELL

The Sunflower

Bring me the sunflower and I'll transplant
it in my garden's burnt salinity.
All day its heliocentric gold face
will turn towards the blue of sky and sea.

Things out of darkness incline to the light,
colours flow into music and ascend,
and in that act consume themselves, to burn
is both a revelation and an end.

Bring me that flower whose one aspiration
is to salute the blond shimmering height
where all matter's transformed into essence,
its radial clockface feeding on the light.

EUGENIO MONTALE (1889–1981)

English version by JEREMY REED

Architecture

The architecture of an aunt
Made the child dream of cupolas,
Domes, other smoothly rondured shapes.
Geometries troubled his sleep.

The architecture of young women
Mildly obsessed the young man:
Its globosity, firmness, texture,
Lace cobwebs for adornment and support.

Miles from his aunt, the old child
Watched domes and cupolas defaced
In a hundred countries, as time passed.

A thousand kilometres of lace defiled,
And much gleaming and perfect architecture
Flaming in the fields with no visible support.

DOM MORAES (1938–2004)

The Loch Ness Monster's Song

Sssnnnwhuffffll?
Hnwhuffl hhnnwfl hnfl hfl?
Gdroblboblhobngbl gbl gl g g g g glbgl.
Drublhaflablhaflubhafgabhaflhafl fl fl –
gm grawwwww grf grawf awfgm graw gm.
Hovoplodok-doplodovok-plovodokot-doplodokosh?
Splgraw fok fok splgrafhatchgabrlgabrl fok splfok!
Zgra kra gka fok!
Grof grawff gahf?
Gombl mbl bl –
blm plm,
blm plm,
blm plm,
blp.

EDWIN MORGAN (b. 1920)

199

Inside My Zulu Hut

It is a hive
without any bees
to build the walls
with golden bricks of honey.
A cave cluttered
with a millstone,
calabashes of sour milk
claypots of foaming beer
sleeping grass mats
wooden head rests
tanned goat skins
tied with *riempies*
to wattle rafters
blackened by the smoke
of kneaded cow dung
burning under
the three-legged pot
on the earthen floor
to cook my porridge.

MBUYISENI MTSHALI (b. 1940)

The Boundary Commission

You remember that village where the border ran
Down the middle of the street,
With the butcher and baker in different states?
Today he remarked how a shower of rain

Had stopped so cleanly across Golightly's lane
It might have been a wall of glass
That had toppled over. He stood there, for ages,
To wonder which side, if any, he should be on.

PAUL MULDOON (b. 1951)

An Old Pit Pony

An old pit pony walks
its chalks
across a blasted heath.

Its coat is a cloud hung on a line.

It sighs
for the pit-propped skies
of that world beneath.

Its coat is a cloud hung on a line.

PAUL MULDOON

Late Summer Fires

The paddocks shave black
with a foam of smoke that stays,
welling out of red-black wounds.

In the white of a drought
this happens. The hardcourt game.
Logs that fume are mostly cattle,

inverted, stubby. Tree stumps are kilns.
Walloped, wiped, hand-pumped,
even this day rolls over, slowly.

At dusk, a family drives sheep
out through the yellow
of the Aboriginal flag.

LES MURRAY (b. 1938)

My Voice

I come from a distant land
with a foreign knapsack on my back
with a silenced song on my lips

As I travelled down the river of my life
I saw my voice
(like Jonah)
swallowed by a whale

And my very life lived in my voice
Kabul, December 1989

PARTAW NADERI (b. 1953)
translated by SARAH MAGUIRE *and* YAMA YARI

from Poetry

And it was at that age . . . Poetry arrived
in search of me. I don't know, I don't know where
it came from, from winter or a river.
I don't know how or when,
no, they were not voices, they were not
words, nor silence,
but from a street I was summoned,
from the branches of night,
abruptly from the others,
among violent fires
or returning alone,
there I was without a face
and it touched me.

PABLO NERUDA (1904–73)

translated by ALASTAIR REID

Like a Beacon

In London
every now and then
I get this craving
for my mother's food
I leave art galleries
in search of plantains
saltfish/sweet potatoes

I need this link

I need this touch
of home
swinging my bag
like a beacon
against the cold

GRACE NICHOLS (b. 1950)

Epilogue

I have crossed an ocean
I have lost my tongue
from the root of the old one
a new one has sprung

GRACE NICHOLS

The River Road

Come for a walk down the river road,
For though you're all a long time dead
The waters part to let us pass

The way we'd go on summer nights
In the times we were children
And thought we were lovers.

The river road led to the end of it all –
Stones and pale water, the lightship's bell
And distance we never looked into.

A long time gone
And the river road with it.
No margin to keep us in mind.

For afterlife, only beginning, beginning,
Wide, dark waters that grow in the telling,
Where the river road carries us now.

SEAN O'BRIEN (b. 1952)

Animals

Have you forgotten what we were like then
when we were still first rate
and the day came fat with an apple in its mouth

it's no use worrying about Time
but we did have a few tricks up our sleeves
and turned some sharp corners

the whole pasture looked like our meal
we didn't need speedometers
we could manage cocktails out of ice and water

I wouldn't want to be faster
or greener than now if you were with me O you
were the best of all my days

FRANK O'HARA (1926–66)

I Sing of Change

I sing
of the beauty of Athens
without its slaves

Of a world free
of kings and queens
and other remnants
of an arbitrary past

Of earth
with no sharp north
or deep south
without blind curtains
or iron walls

Of the end
of warlords and armouries
and prisons of hate and fear

Of deserts treeing
and fruiting
after the quickening rains

Of the sun radiating ignorance
and stars informing
nights of unknowing

I sing of a world reshaped

NIYI OSUNDARE (b. 1947)

Wedding

From time to time our love is like a sail
and when the sail begins to alternate
from tack to tack, it's like a swallowtail
and when the swallow flies it's like a coat;
and if the coat is yours, it has a tear
like a wide mouth and when the mouth begins
to draw the wind, it's like a trumpeter
and when the trumpet blows, it blows like millions . . .
and this, my love, when millions come and go
beyond the need of us, is like a trick;
and when the trick begins, it's like a toe
tip-toeing on a rope, which is like luck;
and when the luck begins, it's like a wedding,
which is like love, which is like everything.

ALICE OSWALD (b. 1966)

Anthem for Doomed Youth

What passing-bells for these who die as cattle?
　　– Only the monstrous anger of the guns.
　　Only the stuttering rifles' rapid rattle
Can patter out their hasty orisons.
No mockeries now for them; no prayers nor bells;
　　Nor any voice of mourning save the choirs, –
The shrill demented choirs of wailing shells;
　　And bugles calling for them from sad shires.

What candles may be held to speed them all?
　　Not in the hands of boys, but in their eyes
Shall shine the holy glimmers of goodbyes.
　　The pallor of girls' brows shall be their pall;
Their flowers the tenderness of patient minds,
And each slow dusk a drawing-down of blinds.

WILFRED OWEN (1893–1918)

Misty

How I love

The darkwave music
Of a sun's eclipse
You can't see for cloud

The saxophonist playing 'Misty'
In the High Street outside Barclays

Accompanied by mating-calls
Sparked off
In a Jaguar alarm

The way you're always there
Where I'm thinking

Or several beats ahead.

RUTH PADEL (b. 1947)

'Loving the rituals'

Loving the rituals that keep men close,
Nature created means for friends apart:

pen, paper, ink, the alphabet,
signs for the distant and disconsolate heart.

PALLADAS (4th century AD)

translated by TONY HARRISON

The Flaw in Paganism

Drink and dance and laugh and lie,
  Love, the reeling midnight through,
For tomorrow we shall die!
  (But, alas, we never do.)

DOROTHY PARKER (1893–1967)

The Algonquin Round Table Dorothy Parker (lower left) surrounded by
Robert Benchley, Alfred Lunt and Lynn Fontanne, Frank Crowninshield,
Alexander Woollcott, Heywood Broun, Marc Connelly, Frank Case, Franklin
P. Adams, Edna Ferber, George Kaufman and Robert Sherwood.

Illustration by Al Hirschfeld.

Tin Roof

Wild harmattan winds whip you
but still you stay;
they spit dust all over your gleam
and twist your sharp cutting edges.
The rains come zinging mud
with their own tapping music
yet you remain
– my pride –
my very own tin roof.

NII AYIKWEI PARKES (b. 1974)

Road

Traveller, your footprints are
the only path, the only track:
wayfarer, there is no way,
there is no map or Northern star,
just a blank page and a starless dark;
and should you turn round to admire
the distance that you've made today
the road will billow into dust.
No way on and no way back,
there is no way, my comrade: trust
your own quick step, the end's delay,
the vanished trail of your own wake,
wayfarer, sea-walker, Christ.

DON PATERSON (b. 1963)

Song

Whenas the rye reach to the chin,
And chopcherry, chopcherry ripe within,
Strawberries swimming in the cream,
And schoolboys playing in the stream:
Then O, then O, then O, my true love said,
Till that time come again,
She could not live a maid.

from THE OLD WIVES' TALE

GEORGE PEELE (1556–96)

Fenland Station in Winter

The railway station in winter lies wide open on three sides;
A waiting mousetrap.
No creatures out in the hard fields,
The desert of blue-lipped ice.
The tracks tweeze the last thin train away,
Wipe it on the rim, and lose it.

The sky is bent so low now, the wind is horizontal.
It whittles the sky's undersurface to the pith,
Paring away a grey unwinding peel of snow.
A mean, needling flake rides the flat wind,
Picking the empty teeth of the trees,
Then falling, frantic, to gnaw at the setting earth,
Clinging there like a starving mouse's claws in velvet.

KATHERINE PIERPOINT (b. 1961)

A Song

Lying is an occupation
  Used by all who mean to rise;
Politicians owe their station
  But to well-concerted lies.

These to lovers give assistance,
  To ensnare the fair one's heart;
And the virgin's best resistance
  Yields to this commanding art.

Study this superior science,
  Would you rise in church or state;
Bid to truth a bold defiance,
  'Tis the practice of the great.

LAETITIA PILKINGTON (1708–50)

Child

Your clear eye is the one absolutely beautiful thing.
I want to fill it with colour and ducks,
The zoo of the new

Whose names you meditate –
April snowdrop, Indian pipe,
Little

Stalk without wrinkle,
Pool in which images
Should be grand and classical

Not this troublous
Wringing of hands, this dark
Ceiling without a star.

SYLVIA PLATH (1932–63)

The Red Cockatoo

Sent as a present from Annam –
A red cockatoo.
Coloured like the peach-tree blossom,
Speaking with the speech of men.

And they did to it what is always done
To the learned and eloquent.
They took a cage with stout bars
And shut it up inside.

PO CHÜ-I (AD 772–846)
translated by ARTHUR WALEY

Calligraphy by Qu Lei Lei

Belgrade

White bone among the clouds

You arise out of your pyre
Out of your ploughed-up barrows
Out of your scattered ashes

You arise out of your disappearance

The sun keeps you
In its golden reliquary
High above the yapping of centuries

And bears you to the marriage
Of the fourth river of Paradise
With the thirty-sixth river of Earth

White bone among the clouds
Bone of our bones

VASCO POPA (1922–91)
translated from the Serbo-Croat by ANNE PENNINGTON

Waiting for Rain in Devon

Rain here on a tableau of cows
might seem a return to everyday –
why, you can almost poach
the trout with your hands,
their element has so thickened!
Something has emerged from dreams
to show us where we are going,
a journey to a desolate star.
Come back, perennial rain,
stand your soft sculptures in our gardens
for the barefoot frogs to leap.

PETER PORTER (1929–2010)

Sometimes

Sometimes things don't go, after all,
from bad to worse. Some years, muscadel
faces down frost; green thrives; the crops don't fail,
sometimes a man aims high, and all goes well.

A people sometimes will step back from war;
elect an honest man; decide they care
enough, that they can't leave some stranger poor.
Some men become what they were born for.

Sometimes our best efforts do not go
amiss; sometimes we do as we meant to.
The sun will sometimes melt a field of sorrow
that seemed hard frozen: may it happen for you.

SHEENAGH PUGH (b. 1950)

Dream

I am become a stranger to my dreams,
Their places unknown. A bridge there was
Over the lovely waters of the Tyne, my mother
Was with me, we were almost there,
It seemed, but in that almost opened up a valley
Extending and expanding, wind-sculptured sand;
Dry its paths, a beautiful waterless waste
Without one green leaf, sand-coloured behind closed eyes.
That film shifts, but the arid place remains
When day returns. Yet we were still going towards the Tyne,
That green river-side where childhood's flowers
Were growing still, my mother and I, she dead,
With me for ever in that dream.

KATHLEEN RAINE (1908–2003)

Birch Canoe

Red men embraced   my body's whiteness,
cutting into me   carved it free,
sewed it tight   with sinews taken
from lightfoot deer   who leaped this stream –
now in my ghost-skin   they glide over clouds
at home in the fish's   fallen heaven.

CARTER REVARD (b. 1931)

Aunt Jennifer's Tigers

Aunt Jennifer's tigers prance across a screen,
Bright topaz denizens of a world of green.
They do not fear the men beneath the tree;
They pace in sleek chivalric certainty.

Aunt Jennifer's fingers fluttering through her wool
Find even the ivory needle hard to pull.
The massive weight of Uncle's wedding band
Sits heavily upon Aunt Jennifer's hand.

When Aunt is dead, her terrified hands will lie
Still ringed with ordeals she was mastered by.
The tigers in the panel that she made
Will go on prancing, proud and unafraid.

ADRIENNE RICH (b. 1929)

Expectans Expectavi

The candid freezing season again:
Candle and cracker, needles of fir and frost;
Carols that through the night air pass, piercing
The glassy husk of heart and heaven;
Children's faces white in the pane, bright in the tree-light.

And the waiting season again,
That begs a crust and suffers joy vicariously:
In bodily starvation now, in the spirit's exile always.
O might the hilarious reign of love begin, let in
Like carols from the cold
The lost who crowd the pane, numb outcasts into welcome.

ANNE RIDLER (1912–2001)

Miracle

A man, before going to bed, put his watch under his pillow.
Then he went to sleep. Outside the wind was blowing. You
  who know
the miraculous continuity of little motions, understand.
A man, his watch, the wind. Nothing else.

YANNIS RITSOS (1909–90)

translated by RAE DALVEN

New Gravity

Treading through the half-light of ivy
and headstone, I see you in the distance
as I'm telling our daughter
about this place, this whole business:
a sister about to be born,
how a life's new gravity suspends in water.
Under the oak, the fallen leaves
are pieces of the tree's jigsaw;
by your father's grave you are pressing acorns
into the shadows to seed.

ROBIN ROBERTSON (b. 1955)

Nasturtium Scanned

Ropey, lippy, loopy, scribbly
over a brick's edge,
she's a riot,
straggly as random and tricky as a diet,
tiddly, wobbly, oddly nibbly
and flashy as a landmine on her vine-meandrine
Alexandrine tangle-scanned line.

JUDITH RODRIGUEZ (b. 1936)

Dolor

I have known the inexorable sadness of pencils,
Neat in their boxes, dolor of pad and paper-weight,
All the misery of manilla folders and mucilage,
Desolation in immaculate public places,
Lonely reception room, lavatory, switchboard,
The unalterable pathos of basin and pitcher,
Ritual of multigraph, paper-clip, comma,
Endless duplication of lives and objects.
And I have seen dust from the walls of institutions,
Finer than flour, alive, more dangerous than silica,
Sift, almost invisible, through long afternoons of tedium,
Dropping a fine film on nails and delicate eyebrows,
Glazing the pale hair, the duplicate grey standard faces.

THEODORE ROETHKE (1908–63)

August 1914

What in our lives is burnt
In the fire of this?
The heart's dear granary?
The much we shall miss?

Three lives hath one life –
Iron, honey, gold.
The gold, the honey gone –
Left is the hard and cold.

Iron are our lives
Molten right through our youth.
A burnt space through ripe fields,
A fair mouth's broken tooth.

ISAAC ROSENBERG (1890–1918)

A Birthday

My heart is like a singing bird
   Whose nest is in a watered shoot;
My heart is like an apple-tree
   Whose boughs are bent with thick-set fruit;
My heart is like a rainbow shell
   That paddles in a halcyon sea;
My heart is gladder than all these
   Because my love is come to me.

Raise me a dais of silk and down;
   Hang it with vair and purple dyes;
Carve it in doves and pomegranates,
   And peacocks with a hundred eyes;
Work it in gold and silver grapes,
   In leaves and silver fleurs-de-lys;
Because the birthday of my life
   Is come, my love is come to me.

CHRISTINA ROSSETTI (1830–94)

Two Fragments

Love holds me captive again
and I tremble with bittersweet longing

As a gale on the mountainside bends the oak tree
I am rocked by my love

SAPPHO (fl. 600 BC)
translated by CICELY HERBERT

Once

after 'Ya Vas Liubil' by Alexander Pushkin

I loved you once. D'you hear a small '*I love you*'
   Each time we're forced to meet? Don't groan, don't hide!
A damaged tree can live without a bud:
   No one need break the branches and uncover
The green that should have danced, dying inside.
   I loved you, knowing I'd never be your lover.
And now? I wish you summers of leaf-shine
   And leaf-shade, and a face in dreams above you,
   As tender and as innocent as mine.
                         'Rogue Translations No. 1'

CAROL RUMENS (b. 1944)

A song for England

An' a so de rain a-fall
An' a so de snow a-rain

An' a so de fog a-fall
An' a so de sun a-fail

An' a so de seasons mix
An' a so de bag-o'-tricks

But a so me understan'
De misery o' de Englishman.

ANDREW SALKEY (1928–95)

Grass

Pile the bodies high at Austerlitz and Wa
Shovel them under and let me work –
      I am the grass; I cov

And pile them high at Gettysburg
And pile them high at Ypres and Verdu
Shovel them under and let me work.
Two years, ten years, and passengers a
      What place is this?
      Where are we now

   I am the grass.
   Let me work.

CARL SANDBURG (1878–196

A Glass of Water

Here is a glass of water from my well.
It tastes of rock and root and earth and rain;
It is the best I have, my only spell,
And it is cold, and better than champagne.
Perhaps someone will pass this house one day
To drink, and be restored, and go his way,
Someone in dark confusion as I was
When I drank down cold water in a glass,
Drank a transparent health to keep me sane,
After the bitter mood had gone again.

MAY SARTON (1912–95)

Everyone Sang

Everyone suddenly burst out singing;
And I was filled with such delight
As prisoned birds must find in freedom,
Winging wildly across the white
Orchards and dark-green fields; on – on – and out of sight.

Everyone's voice was suddenly lifted;
And beauty came like the setting sun:
My heart was shaken with tears; and horror
Drifted away . . . O, but Everyone
Was a bird; and the song was wordless; the singing will
    never be done.

April 1919

SIEGFRIED SASSOON (1886–1967)

Day Trip

Two women, seventies, hold hands
on the edge of Essex,
hair in strong nets,
shrieked laughter echoing gulls
as shingle sucks from under feet
easing in brine.

There must be an unspoken point
when the sea feels like
their future. No longer paddling,
ankles submerge in lace,
in satin ripple.
Dress hems darken.

They do not risk their balance
for the shimmering of ships
at the horizon's sweep
as, thigh deep, they inch on
fingers splayed, wrists bent,
learning to walk again.

CAROLE SATYAMURTI (b. 1939)

And Now Goodbye

To all those million verses in the world
I've added just a few.
They probably were no wiser than a cricket's chirrup.
I know. Forgive me.
I'm coming to the end.

They weren't even the first footmarks
in the lunar dust.
If at times they sparkled after all
it was not their light.
I loved this language.

And that which forces silent lips
to quiver
will make young lovers kiss
as they stroll through red-gilded fields
under a sunset
slower than in the tropics.

Poetry is with us from the start.
Like loving,
like hunger, like the plague, like war.
At times my verses were embarrassingly foolish.

But I make no excuse.
I believe that seeking beautiful words
is better
than killing and murdering.

JAROSLAV SEIFERT (1901–86)
translated from the Czech by EWALD OSERS

Nocturne

And we shall bathe, my love, in the presence of Africa.
Furnishings from Guinea and the Congo, heavy and
   burnished, calm and dark.
Masks, pure and primeval, on the walls, distant but
   so present!
Ebony thrones for ancestral guests, the Princes of the
   hill country.
Musky perfumes, thick grass-mats of silence,
Shadowed cushions for leisure, the sound of a spring –
   of peace.
Mythic language; and far-off songs, voices woven like
   the strip-cloths of the Sudan.
And then, dear lamp, your kindness in cradling the
   obsession with this presence,
Black, white, and red: oh! red like the earth of Africa.

LÉOPOLD SÉDAR SENGHOR (1906–2001)
translated by GERARD BENSON

Guinep

Our mothers have a thing
about guinep:

Mind you don't eat guinep in your good clothes.
It will stain them.

Mind you don't climb guinep tree.
You will fall.

Mind you don't swallow guinep seed.
It will grow inside you.

Our mothers have a thing
about guinep: they're
secretly consuming it.

OLIVE SENIOR (b. 1943)

Guinep Illustration by
permission of the Natural
History Museum.

Sonnet 18

Shall I compare thee to a summer's day?
Thou art more lovely and more temperate:
Rough winds do shake the darling buds of May,
And summer's lease hath all too short a date:
Sometime too hot the eye of heaven shines,
And often is his gold complexion dimmed;
And every fair from fair sometime declines,
By chance, or nature's changing course, untrimmed;
But thy eternal summer shall not fade,
Nor lose possession of that fair thou owest,
Nor shall death brag thou wander'st in his shade,
When in eternal lines to time thou growest;
 So long as men can breathe, or eyes can see,
 So long lives this, and this gives life to thee.

WILLIAM SHAKESPEARE (1564–1616)

Feste's Song

O mistress mine, where are you roaming?
O, stay and hear: your true love's coming,
   That can sing both high and low.
Trip no further, pretty sweeting;
Journeys end in lovers meeting,
   Every wise man's son doth know.

What is love? 'tis not hereafter;
Present mirth hath present laughter;
   What's to come is still unsure:
In delay there lies no plenty;
Then come kiss me, sweet and twenty,
   Youth's a stuff will not endure.

from TWELFTH NIGHT

WILLIAM SHAKESPEARE

Sonnet 73

That time of year thou mayst in me behold
When yellow leaves, or none, or few, do hang
Upon those boughs which shake against the cold,
Bare ruined choirs, where late the sweet birds sang.
In me thou seest the twilight of such day
As after sunset fadeth in the west;
Which by and by black night doth take away,
Death's second self, that seals up all in rest.
In me thou seest the glowing of such fire,
That on the ashes of his youth doth lie,
As the deathbed whereon it must expire,
Consumed with that which it was nourished by.
  This thou perceiv'st, which makes thy love more strong,
  To love that well, which thou must leave ere long.

WILLIAM SHAKESPEARE

'Fear no more the heat o' the sun'

Fear no more the heat o' the sun,
   Nor the furious winter's rages;
Thou thy worldly task hast done,
   Home art gone, and ta'en thy wages.
Golden lads and girls all must,
As chimney-sweepers, come to dust.

Fear no more the frown o' the great;
   Thou art past the tyrant's stroke;
Care no more to clothe and eat;
   To thee the reed is as the oak.
The sceptre, learning, physic, must
All follow this, and come to dust.

Fear no more the lightning flash,
   Nor th' all-dreaded thunder stone;
Fear not slander, censure rash;
   Thou hast finished joy and moan.
All lovers young, all lovers must
Consign to thee, and come to dust.

No exorciser harm thee!
Nor no witchcraft charm thee!
Ghost unlaid forbear thee!
Nothing ill come near thee!
Quiet consummation have;
And renowned be thy grave!

from CYMBELINE

WILLIAM SHAKESPEARE

Quark

'Transcendental,' said the technician,
'to stumble on a quark that talks back.
I will become a mystagogue, initiate
punters into the wonder of it for cash.'
'Bollocks,' said the quark, from its aluminium
nacelle. 'I don't need no dodgy
crypto-human strategising my future.
Gonna down-size under the cocoplum
or champak, drink blue marimbas into
the sunset, and play with speaking quarklike
while I beflower the passing gravitons.'

JO SHAPCOTT (b. 1953)

Swallows

The swallows are italic again,
cutting their sky-jive
between the telephone wires,
flying in crossed lines.

Their annual regeneration
so flawless to human eyes
that there is no seam
between parent and child.

Just always the swallows
and their script of descenders,
dipping their ink to sign their signatures
across the page of the sky.

OWEN SHEERS (b. 1974)

Ozymandias

I met a traveller from an antique land
Who said: Two vast and trunkless legs of stone
Stand in the desert . . . Near them, on the sand,
Half sunk, a shattered visage lies, whose frown,
And wrinkled lip, and sneer of cold command,
Tell that its sculptor well those passions read
Which yet survive, stamped on these lifeless things,
The hand that mocked them and the heart that fed;
And on the pedestal these words appear:
'My name is OZYMANDIAS, king of kings:
Look on my works, ye Mighty, and despair!'
Nothing beside remains. Round the decay
Of that colossal wreck, boundless and bare
The lone and level sands stretch far away.

PERCY BYSSHE SHELLEY (1792–1822)

To Emilia V –

Music, when soft voices die,
Vibrates in the memory –
Odours, when sweet violets sicken,
Live within the sense they quicken.

Rose leaves, when the rose is dead,
Are heaped for the beloved's bed –
And so thy thoughts, when thou art gone,
Love itself shall slumber on . . .

PERCY BYSSHE SHELLEY

A True and Faithful Inventory
of the Goods *belonging* to Dr. Swift,
Vicar of *Lara Cor*;

upon lending his House to the Bishop of Meath,
until his own was built

An Oaken, broken, Elbow-Chair;
A Cawdle-Cup, without an Ear;
A batter'd, shatter'd Ash Bedstead;
A Box of Deal, without a Lid;
A Pair of Tongs, but out of Joint;
A Back-Sword Poker, without Point;
A Pot that's crack'd across, around,
With an old knotted Garter bound;
An iron lock, without a Key;
A Wig, with hanging, quite grown grey;
A Curtain worn to Half a Stripe;
A Pair of Bellows, without Pipe;
A Dish, which might good Meat afford once;
An *Ovid*, and an old *Concordance*;
A Bottle Bottom, Wooden Platter,
One is for Meal, and one for Water:
There likewise is a Copper Skillet,
Which runs as fast out as you fill it;
A Candlestick, Snuff dish, and Save-all,
And thus his Household Goods you have all.
These, to your Lordship, as a Friend,
Till you have built, I freely lend:
They'll save your Lordship for a Shift;
Why not, as well as Doctor *Swift*?

THOMAS SHERIDAN (1687–1738)

My true love hath my heart and I have his,
By just exchange one for the other given.
I hold his dear, and mine he cannot miss,
There never was a better bargain driven.
    My true love hath my heart and I have his.

His heart in me keeps me and him in one,
My heart in him his thoughts and senses guides:
He loves my heart, for once it was his own,
I cherish his because in me it bides.
    My true love hath my heart, and I have his.

SIR PHILIP SIDNEY (1554–86)

The silver swan, who living had no note,
When death approached unlocked her silent throat,
Leaning her breast against the reedy shore,
Thus sung her first and last, and sung no more:
Farewell all joys, O death come close mine eyes,
More geese than swans now live, more fools than wise.

ANON. (*c.* 1600)

'The silver Swanne'   A setting by the court composer Orlando Gibbons of this anonymous elegiac poem, in *The First Set of Madrigals and Mottets* (1612). It has been suggested that the poem may refer to the death of Edmund Spenser, in 1599. BL Royal Mus. 15.e.2 (10). By permission of The British Library Board.

The Exiles

translated from the author's own Gaelic

The many ships that left our country
with white wings for Canada.
They are like handkerchiefs in our memories
and the brine like tears
and in their masts sailors singing
like birds on branches.
That sea of May running in such blue,
a moon at night, a sun at daytime,
and the moon like a yellow fruit,
like a plate on a wall
to which they raise their hands
like a silver magnet
with piercing rays
streaming into the heart.

IAIN CRICHTON SMITH (1928–98)

Encounter at St. Martin's

I tell a wanderer's tale, the same
I began long ago, a boy in a barn,
I am always lost in it. The place
is always strange to me. In my pocket

the wrong money or none, the wrong paper,
maps of another town, the phrase book
for yesterday's language, just a ticket
to the next station, and my instructions.

In the lobby of the Banco Bilbao
a dark woman will slip me a key, a package,
the name of a hotel, a numbered account,
the first letters of an unknown alphabet.

KEN SMITH (1938–2003)

Not Waving but Drowning

Nobody heard him, the dead man,
But still he lay moaning:
I was much further out than you thought
And not waving but drowning.

Poor chap, he always loved larking
And now he's dead
It must have been too cold for him his heart gave way,
They said.

Oh, no no no, it was too cold always
(Still the dead one lay moaning)
I was much too far out all my life
And not waving but drowning.

STEVIE SMITH (1902–71)

Self-portrait of Stevie Smith
From *Collected Poems of Stevie
Smith* (Penguin 20th Century
Classics). By permission of
James MacGibbon.

Two Poems Written at Maple Bridge Near Su-chou

Maple Bridge Night Mooring

Moon set, a crow caws,
     frost fills the sky
River, maple, fishing-fires
     cross my troubled sleep.
Beyond the walls of Su-chou
     from Cold Mountain temple
The midnight bell sounds
     reach my boat.

     (*circa* AD 765)

CHANG CHI (mid-8th century), *translated by* GARY SNYDER

At Maple Bridge

Men are mixing gravel and cement
At Maple bridge,
Down an alley by a tea-stall
From Cold Mountain temple;
Where Chang Chi heard the bell.
The stone step moorage
Empty, lapping water,
And the bell sound has travelled
Far across the sea.

     (AD 1984)

GARY SNYDER (b. 1930)

from The Song of Solomon

My beloved spake, and said unto me, Rise up, my love, my fair
    one, and come away.
For lo, the winter is past, the rain is over, and gone.
The flowers appear on the earth, the time of the singing of
    birds is come, and the voice of the turtle is heard in our
    land.
The fig tree putteth forth her green figs, and the vines with
    the tender grape give a good smell.
Arise, my love, my fair one, and come away.

THE KING JAMES BIBLE (1611)

Season

Rust is ripeness, rust,
And the wilted corn-plume;
Pollen is mating-time when swallows
Weave a dance
Of feathered arrows
Thread corn-stalks in winged
Streaks of light. And, we loved to hear
Spliced phrases of the wind, to hear
Rasps in the field, where corn-leaves
Pierce like bamboo slivers.

Now, garnerers we
Awaiting rust on tassels, draw
Long shadows from the dusk, wreathe
Dry thatch in wood-smoke. Laden stalks
Ride the germ's decay – we await
The promise of the rust.

WOLE SOYINKA (b. 1935)

To My Daughter

Bright clasp of her whole hand around my finger
My daughter, as we walk together now.
All my life I'll feel a ring invisibly
Circle this bone with shining: when she is grown
Far from today as her eyes are far already.

STEPHEN SPENDER (1909–95)

Disillusionment of Ten O'Clock

The houses are haunted
By white night-gowns.
None are green,
Or purple with green rings,
Or green with yellow rings,
Or yellow with blue rings.
None of them are strange,
With socks of lace
And beaded ceintures.
People are not going
To dream of baboons and periwinkles.
Only, here and there, an old sailor,
Drunk and asleep in his boots,
Catches tigers
In red weather.

WALLACE STEVENS (1879–1955)

Lesson

The girls and boys in winter know
That love is like the drifting snow;
It praises everything although
Its perishable breath must go.

ANNE STEVENSON (b. 1933)

Ragwort

They won't let railways alone, those yellow flowers.
They're that remorseless joy of dereliction
darkest banks exhale like vivid breath
as bricks divide to let them root between.
How every falling place concocts their smile,
taking what's left and making a song of it.

ANNE STEVENSON

Where Go the Boats?

Dark brown is the river,
 Golden is the sand.
It flows along for ever,
 With trees on either hand.

Green leaves a-floating,
 Castles of the foam,
Boats of mine a-boating –
 Where will all come home?

On goes the river
 And out past the mill,
Away down the valley,
 Away down the hill.

Away down the river,
 A hundred miles or more,
Other little children
 Shall bring my boats ashore.

ROBERT LOUIS STEVENSON (1850–94)

Where Go the Boats?   Illustrations by A.H. Watson from
A Child's Garden of Verses, Collins (1946).

'Sumer is icumen in'

Sumer is icumen in,
Loud sing cuckoo!
Groweth seed and bloweth mead
And springeth the wood now.
Sing cuckoo!

Ewe bleateth after lamb,
Cow loweth after calf,
Bullock starteth, buck farteth,
Merry sing cuckoo!

Cuckoo, cuckoo!
Well singest thou cuckoo,
Nor cease thou never now!

Sing cuckoo now, sing cuckoo!
Sing cuckoo, sing cuckoo now!

ANON. (13th century)

A Tune

A foolish rhythm turns in my idle head
As a wind-mill turns in the wind on an empty sky.
Why is it when love, which men call deathless, is dead,
That memory, men call fugitive, will not die?
Is love not dead? Yet I hear that tune if I lie
Dreaming awake in the night on my lonely bed,
And an old thought turns with the old tune in my head
As a wind-mill turns in the wind on an empty sky.

ARTHUR SYMONS (1865–1945)

Accordionist

for André Kertesz

The accordionist is a blind intellectual
carrying an enormous typewriter whose keys
grow wings as the instrument expands into a tall
horizontal hat that collapses with a tubercular wheeze.

My century is a sad one of collapses.
The concertina of the chest; the tubular bells
of the high houses; the flattened ellipses
of our skulls that open like petals.

We are the poppies sprinkled along the field.
We are simple crosses dotted with blood.
Beware the sentiments concealed
in this short rhyme. Be wise. Be good.

GEORGE SZIRTES (b. 1948)

The Two Apes of Brueghel

Here's my dream of a final exam:
two apes, in chains, sitting at a window.
Outside the sky is flying
and the sea bathes.

I am taking the test on human history.
I stammer and blunder.

One ape, staring at me, listens with irony,
the other seems to doze –
but when I am silent after a question,
she prompts me
with a soft clanking of the chain.

WISŁAWA SZYMBORSKA (b. 1923)

translated by GRAZYNA DRABIK *with* SHARON OLDS

Song

   Now sleeps the crimson petal, now the white;
Nor waves the cypress in the palace walk;
Nor winks the gold fin in the porphyry font:
The fire-fly wakens: waken thou with me.

   Now droops the milkwhite peacock like a ghost,
And like a ghost she glimmers on to me.

   Now lies the Earth all Danaë to the stars,
And all thy heart lies open unto me.

   Now slides the silent meteor on, and leaves
A shining furrow, as thy thoughts in me.

   Now folds the lily all her sweetness up,
And slips into the bosom of the lake:
So fold thyself, my dearest, thou, and slip
Into my bosom and be lost in me.

from THE PRINCESS

ALFRED, LORD TENNYSON (1809–92)

In my Craft or Sullen Art

In my craft or sullen art
Exercised in the still night
When only the moon rages
And the lovers lie abed
With all their griefs in their arms,
I labour by singing light
Not for ambition or bread
Or the strut and trade of charms
On the ivory stages
But for the common wages
Of their most secret heart.

Not for the proud man apart
From the raging moon I write
On these spindrift pages
Nor for the towering dead
With their nightingales and psalms
But for the lovers, their arms
Round the griefs of the ages,
Who pay no praise or wages
Nor heed my craft or art.

DYLAN THOMAS (1914–53)

Do Not Go Gentle Into That Good Night

Do not go gentle into that good night,
Old age should burn and rave at close of day;
Rage, rage against the dying of the light.

Though wise men at their end know dark is right,
Because their words had forked no lightning they
Do not go gentle into that good night.

Good men, the last wave by, crying how bright
Their frail deeds might have danced in a green bay,
Rage, rage against the dying of the light.

Wild men who caught and sang the sun in flight,
And learn, too late, they grieved it on its way,
Do not go gentle into that good night.

Grave men, near death, who see with blinding sight
Blind eyes could blaze like meteors and be gay,
Rage, rage against the dying of the light.

And you, my father, there on the sad height,
Curse, bless, me now with your fierce tears, I pray.
Do not go gentle into that good night.
Rage, rage against the dying of the light.

DYLAN THOMAS

Snow

In the gloom of whiteness,
In the great silence of snow,
A child was sighing
And bitterly saying: 'Oh,
They have killed a white bird up there on her nest,
The down is fluttering from her breast!'
And still it fell through that dusky brightness
On the child crying for the bird of the snow.

EDWARD THOMAS (1878–1917)

The Ancients of the World

The salmon lying in the depths of Llyn Llifon,
    Secretly as a thought in a dark mind,
Is not so old as the owl of Cwm Cowlyd
    Who tells her sorrow nightly on the wind.

The ousel singing in the woods of Cilgwri,
    Tirelessly as a stream over the mossed stones,
Is not so old as the toad of Cors Fochno
    Who feels the cold skin sagging round his bones.

The toad and the ousel and the stag of Rhedynfre,
    That has cropped each leaf from the tree of life,
Are not so old as the owl of Cwm Cowlyd,
    That the proud eagle would have to wife.

R.S. THOMAS (1913–2000)

At Lord's

It is little I repair to the matches of the Southron folk,
    Though my own red roses there may blow;
It is little I repair to the matches of the Southron folk,
    Though the red roses crest the caps, I know.
For the field is full of shades as I near the shadowy coast,
And a ghostly batsman plays to the bowling of a ghost,
And I look through my tears on a soundless-clapping host
    As the run-stealers flicker to and fro,
        To and fro: –
O my Hornby and my Barlow long ago!

FRANCIS THOMPSON (1859–1907)

If Bach Had Been a Beekeeper

for Arvo Pärt

If Bach had been a beekeeper
he would have heard
all those notes
suspended above one another
in the air of his ear
as the differentiated swarm returning
to the exact hive
and place in the hive,
topping up the cells
with the honey of C major,
food for the listening generations,
key to their comfort
and solace of their distress
as they return and return
to those counterpointed levels
of hovering wings where
movement is dance
and the air itself
a scented garden

CHARLES TOMLINSON (b. 1927)

From March '79

Tired of all who come with words, words but no language
I went to the snow-covered island.
The wild does not have words.
The unwritten pages spread themselves out in all directions!
I come across the marks of roe-deer's hooves in the snow.
Language but no words.

TOMAS TRANSTRÖMER (b. 1931)
translated by JOHN F. DEANE

'I know the truth – give up all other truths!'

I know the truth – give up all other truths!
No need for people anywhere on earth to struggle.
Look – it is evening, look, it is nearly night:
what do you speak of, poets, lovers, generals?

The wind is level now, the earth is wet with dew,
the storm of stars in the sky will turn to quiet.
And soon all of us will sleep under the earth, we
who never let each other sleep above it.

1915

MARINA TSVETAYEVA (1892–1941)
translated by ELAINE FEINSTEIN

The Twa Corbies

As I was walking all alane,
I heard twa corbies making a mane;
The tane unto the tither say,
'Whar sall we gang and dine the day?'

'In behint yon auld fail dyke,
I wot there lies a new-slain knight;
And naebody kens that he lies there,
But his hawk, his hound, and lady fair.

'His hound is to the hunting gane,
His hawk to fetch the wild-fowl hame,
His lady's ta'en another mate,
Sae we may mak our dinner sweet.

'Ye'll sit on his white hause-bane,
And I'll pike out his bonnie blue een:
Wi' ae lock o' his gowden hair
We'll theek our nest when it grows bare.

'Mony a one for him makes mane,
But nane sall ken whar he is gane;
O'er his white banes, when they are bare,
The wind sall blaw for evermair.'

ANON. (before 1800)

corbie: raven   *mane:* moan   *hause-bane:* neck-bone

Midsummer, Tobago

Broad sun-stoned beaches.

White heat.
A green river.

A bridge,
scorched yellow palms

from the summer-sleeping house
drowsing through August.

Days I have held,
days I have lost,

days that outgrow, like daughters,
my harbouring arms.

DEREK WALCOTT (b. 1930)

Map of the New World: Archipelagoes

At the end of this sentence, rain will begin.
At the rain's edge, a sail.

Slowly the sail will lose sight of islands;
into a mist will go the belief in harbours
of an entire race.

The ten-years war is finished.
Helen's hair, a grey cloud.
Troy, a white ashpit
by the drizzling sea.

The drizzle tightens like the strings of a harp.
A man with clouded eyes picks up the rain
and plucks the first line of the *Odyssey*.

DEREK WALCOTT

'Western wind when wilt thou blow'

Western wind when wilt thou blow
the small rain down can rain
Christ if my love were in my arms
and I in my bed again

ANON. (early 16th century)

'Westron wynde when wylt thou blow'   Musical setting in a tenor part-book, dating from the early 16th century, which provides the only known source of this famous lyric. BL Royal MS, Appendix 58, f.5. By permission of The British Library Board.

Reconciliation

Word over all, beautiful as the sky,
Beautiful that war and all its deeds of carnage must in
   time be utterly lost,
That the hands of the sisters Death and Night incessantly
   softly wash again, and ever again, this soil'd world;
For my enemy is dead, a man divine as myself is dead,
I look where he lies white-faced and still in the coffin –
   I draw near,
Bend down and touch lightly with my lips the white face
   in the coffin.

WALT WHITMAN (1819–92)

Symphony in Yellow

An omnibus across the bridge
  Crawls like a yellow butterfly,
  And, here and there, a passer-by
Shows like a little restless midge.

Big barges full of yellow hay
  Are moored against the shadowy wharf,
  And, like a yellow silken scarf,
The thick fog hangs along the quay.

The yellow leaves begin to fade
  And flutter from the Temple elms,
  And at my feet the pale green Thames
Lies like a rod of rippled jade.

OSCAR WILDE (1854–1900)

**Caricature of Oscar Wilde
in a Top Hat**   Black and white
drawing by Beatrice Whistler.
Birnie Philip Bequest. By
permission of The Hunterian
Art Gallery, University of
Glasgow.

Saturday Morning

Everyone who made love the night before
was walking around with flashing red lights
on top of their heads – a white-haired old gentleman,
a red-faced schoolboy, a pregnant woman
who smiled at me from across the street
and gave a little secret shrug,
as if the flashing red light on her head
was a small price to pay for what she knew.

HUGO WILLIAMS (b. 1942)

This Is Just to Say

I have eaten
the plums
that were in
the icebox

and which
you were probably
saving
for breakfast

Forgive me
they were delicious
so sweet
and so cold

WILLIAM CARLOS WILLIAMS (1883–1963)

Composed upon Westminster Bridge, September 3, 1802

Earth has not anything to show more fair:
Dull would he be of soul who could pass by
A sight so touching in its majesty:
This City now doth like a garment wear
The beauty of the morning; silent, bare,
Ships, towers, domes, theatres, and temples lie
Open unto the fields, and to the sky;
All bright and glittering in the smokeless air.
Never did sun more beautifully steep
In his first splendour valley, rock, or hill;
Ne'er saw I, never felt, a calm so deep!
The river glideth at his own sweet will:
Dear God! the very houses seem asleep;
And all that mighty heart is lying still!

WILLIAM WORDSWORTH (1770–1850)

'The world is too much with us'

The world is too much with us; late and soon,
Getting and spending, we lay waste our powers:
Little we see in nature that is ours;
We have given our hearts away, a sordid boon!
This Sea that bares her bosom to the moon;
The Winds that will be howling at all hours
And are up-gathered now like sleeping flowers;
For this, for every thing, we are out of tune;
It moves us not. Great God! I'd rather be
A Pagan suckled in a creed outworn;
So might I, standing on this pleasant lea,
Have glimpses that would make me less forlorn;
Have sight of Proteus rising from the sea;
Or hear old Triton blow his wreathèd horn.

WILLIAM WORDSWORTH

On Himself

Abstracted by silence from the age of seven,
Deafened and penned by as black calamity
As twice to be born, I cannot without pity
Contemplate myself as an infant;

Or fail to speak of silence as a priestess
Calling to serve in the temple of a skull
Her innocent choice. It is barely possible
Not to be affected by such a distress.

DAVID WRIGHT (1920–94)

Rainforest

The forest drips and glows with green.
The tree-frog croaks his far-off song.
His voice is stillness, moss and rain
drunk from the forest ages long.

We cannot understand that call
unless we move into his dream,
where all is one and one is all
and frog and python are the same.

We with our quick dividing eyes
measure, distinguish and are gone.
The forest burns, the tree-frog dies,
yet one is all and all are one.

JUDITH WRIGHT (1915–2000)

Sergeant Brown's Parrot

Many policemen wear upon their shoulders
Cunning little radios. To pass away the time
They talk about the traffic to them, listen to the news,
And it helps them to Keep Down Crime.

But Sergeant Brown, he wears upon his shoulder
A tall green parrot as he's walking up and down
And all the parrot says is 'Who's-a-pretty-boy-then?'
'I am,' says Sergeant Brown.

KIT WRIGHT (b. 1944)

Sergeant Brown's Parrot   Drawing by Posy Simmonds, © Posy
Simmonds. By permission of Collins Publishers.

They Flee from Me

They flee from me that sometime did me seek
With naked foot stalking in my chamber.
I have seen them gentle, tame, and meek
That now are wild, and do not remember
That sometime they put themselves in danger
To take bread at my hand, and now they range,
Busily seeking with a continual change.

Thanked be fortune it hath been otherwise
Twenty times better, but once in special,
In thin array after a pleasant guise
When her loose gown from her shoulders did fall
And she me caught in her arms long and small,
Therewithal sweetly did me kiss
And softly said, Dear heart, how like you this?

It was no dream, I lay broad waking.
But all is turned through my gentleness
Into a strange fashion of forsaking,
And I have leave to go of her goodness,
And she also to use newfangleness.
But since that I so kindly am served,
I would fain know what she hath deserved.

SIR THOMAS WYATT (1503–42)

'Tagus farewell'

Tagus farewell, that westward with thy streams
Turns up the grains of gold already tried:
With spur and sail for I go seek the Thames
Gainward the sun that showeth her wealthy pride
And to the town which Brutus sought by dreams
Like bended moon doth lend her lusty side.
My king, my country, alone for whom I live,
Of mighty love the wings for this me give.

SIR THOMAS WYATT

Tagus: the Spanish and Portuguese river famous for its gold. Wyatt, Ambassador to Spain, was suddenly recalled to London by Henry VIII. The last lines reflect his uneasiness at the fate awaiting him.

Brutus: a descendant of Aeneas, who dreamed that he was destined to found a kingdom in Albion.

Vase

a word eradicates the world
a feather
drifts down

and yet, a bird's nest
in each of its fragments
preserves the whole

YANG LIAN (b. 1955)
translated by JOHN CAYLEY

Her Anxiety

Earth in beauty dressed
Awaits returning spring.
All true love must die,
Alter at the best
Into some lesser thing.
Prove that I lie.

Such body lovers have,
Such exacting breath,
That they touch or sigh.
Every touch they give,
Love is nearer death.
Prove that I lie.

W.B. YEATS (1865–1939)

He wishes for the Cloths of Heaven

Had I the heavens' embroidered cloths,
Enwrought with golden and silver light,
The blue and the dim and the dark cloths
Of night and light and the half-light,
I would spread the cloths under your feet:
But I, being poor, have only my dreams;
I have spread my dreams under your feet;
Tread softly because you tread on my dreams.

W.B. YEATS (1865–1939)

The Lake Isle of Innisfree

I will arise and go now, and go to Innisfree,
And a small cabin build there, of clay and wattles made:
Nine bean-rows will I have there, a hive for the honey-bee,
And live alone in the bee-loud glade.

And I shall have some peace there, for peace comes
    dropping slow,
Dropping from the veils of the morning to where the
    cricket sings;
There midnight's all a glimmer, and noon a purple glow,
And evening full of the linnet's wings.

I will arise and go now, for always night and day
I hear lake water lapping with low sounds by the shore;
While I stand on the roadway, or on the pavements grey,
I hear it in the deep heart's core.

W. B. YEATS

A Prehistoric Camp

It was the time of year
  Pale lambs leap with thick leggings on
Over small hills that are not there,
  That I climbed Eggardon.

The hedgerows still were bare,
  None ever knew so late a year;
Birds built their nests in the open air,
  Love conquering their fear.

But there on the hill-crest,
  Where only larks or stars look down,
Earthworks exposed a vaster nest,
  Its race of men long flown.

ANDREW YOUNG (1885–1971)

Poetry

Who broke these mirrors
and tossed them
shard
by shard
among the branches?
And now . . .
shall we ask L'Akhdar to come and see?
Colours are all muddled up
and the image is entangled
with the thing
and the eyes burn.
L'Akhdar must gather these mirrors
on his palm
and match the pieces together
any way he likes
and preserve
the memory of the branch.

SAADI YOUSSEF (b. 1934)

translated from the Arabic by KHALED MATTAWA

Anti-Slavery Movements

Some people say
Animal liberators are not
Working in the interest of animals.
But I've never seen liberated animals
Protest by going back to their place
Of captivity.
But then again
I've never heard of any liberated slaves
Begging for more humiliation
Or voting for slavery.

Animals vote with their feet
Or their wings
Or their fins.

BENJAMIN ZEPHANIAH (b. 1958)

ACKNOWLEDGEMENTS

The editors and publisher acknowledge permission from copyright holders to reproduce the following copyright poems in this anthology. They would be grateful for notification of any errors or omissions, which will be corrected in future editions.

Dannie Abse: 'Mysteries', from *New and Collected Poems* by Dannie Abse, 2003, published by Hutchinson. Reprinted by permission of The Random House Group Ltd

Fleur Adcock: 'Immigrant', from *Poems 1960-2000*, Bloodaxe Books 2000. Reprinted by permission of Bloodaxe Books

John Agard: 'Don't Call Alligator Long-Mouth till You Cross River', from *Say It Again Granny* (1986), © John Agard 1986. Reprinted by permission of Caroline Sheldon

Patience Agbabi: 'London Eye', from *Bloodshot Monochrome*. First published in Great Britain by Canongate Books Ltd, 14 High Street, Edinburgh, EH1 1TE

Anna Akhmatova: 'Requiem', from *Selected Poems*, Bloodaxe Books 2006, translation © Richard McKane. Reprinted by permission of Bloodaxe Books

Moniza Alvi: 'Indian Cooking', from *Carrying My Wife*, Bloodaxe Books 2000. Reprinted by permission of Bloodaxe Books

Maya Angelou: 'Come. And Be My Baby', from *The Complete Collected Poems* by Maya Angelou (1995), published by Virago, an imprint of Little, Brown Book Group. Reprinted by permission of Little, Brown Book Group.

Simon Armitage: 'The Catch', from *Kid*, © Simon Armitage 1992. Reprinted by permission of Faber and Faber Ltd

W.H. Auden: 'If I Could Tell You'; 'Song' (' Stop all the clocks'), © W.H. Auden 1968, from *Collected Poems, revised edition* (2007). Reprinted by permission of Faber and Faber Ltd

Sebastian Barker: 'In the Heart of Hackney' is from *Damnatio Memoriae: Erased from Memory*, Enitharmon Press, 2004. Reprinted by permission of Enitharmon Press

Bei Dao: 'A Picture' translated by Bonnie McDougall and Chen Maiping, from *Old Snow* (1990), © Bei Dao 1990. Reprinted by permission of Anvil Press Poetry

Connie Bensley: 'Shopper' from *Choosing to be a Swan*, Bloodaxe Books 1994, © Connie Bensley 1994. Reprinted by permission of Bloodaxe Books

Gerard Benson: 'The Coming of Grendel' from *Beowulf*, translation by and © Gerard Benson 1988. Reprinted by permission of the translator

Oliver Bernard: 'Rondel' by Charles d'Orléans, translation by and © Oliver Bernard. Reprinted by permission of the translator. 'Letter to André Billy. 9 April 1915', from *Guillaume Apollinaire: Selected Poems*, translated by Oliver Bernard, published by Anvil Press Poetry 1986, new edition 2004. Reprinted by permission of Anvil Press Poetry

Lorna Goodison: 'I Am Becoming My Mother', from *I Am Becoming My Mother* (1986). Reprinted by permission of New Beacon Press

Robert Graves: 'Love without Hope'; 'She Tells Her Love', from *Complete Poems in One Volume*. Reprinted by permission of Carcanet Press Limited

Lavinia Greenlaw: 'Sisu', from *Minsk*, 2003, © Lavinia Greenlaw 2003. Reprinted by permission of Faber and Faber Ltd

Thom Gunn: 'The Reassurance', from *Collected Poems* (1993). Reprinted by permission of Faber and Faber Ltd

Choman Hardi: 'My children', from *Life for Us*, Bloodaxe Books 2004, © Choman Hardi 2004. Reprinted by permission of Bloodaxe Books

Tony Harrison: 'Loving the Rituals', from *Palladas: Poems* (1975), translation by and © Tony Harrison. Reprinted by permission of the translator

Seamus Heaney: 'The Railway Children', from *Station Island*, © Seamus Heaney 1984; 'The Rescue', from *Seeing Things*, © Seamus Heaney 1991. Reprinted by permission of Faber and Faber Ltd

John Heath-Stubbs: 'The Unpredicted', from *Selected Poems* by John Heath-Stubbs, 2002, published by Carcanet Press. Reprinted by permission of David Higham Associates

John Hegley: 'Into Rail', from *Beyond Our Kennel* (1998). Reprinted by permission of Methuen

Cicely Herbert: 'Everything Changes' © Cicely Herbert 1989. 'Sappho, Two Fragments', translation by and © Cicely Herbert 1993. Reprinted by permission of the author and translator

Geoffrey Hill: 'Merlin', from *Collected Poems*, first published in *For the Unfallen*, 1959, Penguin Books, 1985, © Geoffrey Hill 1959, 1985. Reprinted by permission of Penguin Books

Miroslav Holub: 'Spacetime', translation by and © David Young and Dana Hábová , from *Vanishing Lung Syndrome*, © Miroslav Holub heirs c/o DILIA. Reprinted by permission of DILIA

A.D. Hope: 'The Gateway', from *Selected Poems* (1986), © A.D. Hope 1986. Reprinted by permission of Carcanet Press Limited

Langston Hughes: 'Dream Boogie', from *Collected Poems of Langston Hughes* (1995), published by Alfred A. Knopf Inc. Reprinted by permission of David Higham Associates

Ted Hughes: 'Full Moon and Little Frieda', from *Wodwo*, © Ted Hughes 1982. Reprinted by permission of Faber and Faber Ltd

A.C. Jacobs: 'N.W.2: Spring', from *Collected Poems* (1996). Reprinted by permission of Menard/Hearing Eye/The Estate of A.C. Jacobs

Philippe Jaccottet: 'Distances', translated by Derek Mahon, from *Selected Poems of Philippe Jaccottet*, Penguin Books (1988). Reprinted by permission of the translator and Rogers, Coleridge and White

Kathleen Jamie: 'Rooms', from *Mr and Mrs Scotland are Dead: Poems 1980-1994*, Bloodaxe Books 2002, © Kathleen Jamie 1994. Reprinted by permission of Bloodaxe Books; 'Creel', from *The Tree House*, Picador 1994, © Kathleen Jamie 1994. Reprinted by permission of Pan Macmillan

THE EDITORS

Gerard Benson, poet, editor, performer, taught at the Central School of Speech and Drama for over twenty years. He is the author of ten poetry collections, both for adults and children, most recently his adult collection *A Good Time*, and has edited two Puffin anthologies. He was poet-in-residence at the Wordsworth Trust (the first Dove Cottage poet since Wordsworth himself), and has given many poetry recitals. In 2008 he became the City of Bradford's first Poet Laureate.

Judith Chernaik is the author of *The Lyrics of Shelley* and four novels, most recently *Mab's Daughters*, based on the lives of the Shelley circle. She has published in the *TLS* and other journals, and has written features on Romantic poetry and music for the BBC. Her conversation piece about Mary Shelley and Mary Wollstonecraft, *The Two Marys*, has been widely performed in the UK and abroad. In 2002 she was awarded an OBE for services to literature.

Cicely Herbert is a writer, a performer and a member of the Barrow Poets. She has written several performance pieces with music by Jim Parker; these include *Petticoat Lane*, for BBC TV, and two concert pieces commissioned by the Nash Ensemble, *Scenes from Victorian London* and *La Comédie Humaine*. Her radio play, *Yeats and Margot*, has been broadcast on BBC Radio 4, and her poems for children have been widely anthologised. She writes on arts events for the magazine *Sofia*.